Difficult Relationships In The Workplace

Manage Diversity And Politics, Improve Your Resilience And Strength Effectively, Gain Emotional Intelligence, And Prevent Burnout

Written by

Lucca Zeni

mindfulpersona.com

Table of Contents

Introduction **6**

Chapter One: Working With Different Personalities **15**

Real Meaning of "Surviving" In the Workplace? 16

How Do Coworkers Become Toxic? 19

How Can You Spot Toxic Coworkers? 21

The Seven Personalities at Work 24

Keep Yourself Protected 30

Chapter Two: Changing People's Perception About You + 28 Days Workbook Journal Exercise **33**

People's Perceptions of You at Work 36

The 28 Days Worksheet Journal Exercise 44

How to Tell That Someone Needs Reassurance on The Job 46

Training an Employee Who Requires Reassurance 47

How You Can Motivate Your Workmate Who Needs Reassurance 48

How To Give Feedback To Them 49

Chapter Three: Goal Setting – Building a Foundation for A Better Future **52**

Understanding Long-Term Goals and Their Importance 54

Recognizing Where You Are Currently On Your Career Path And Where You Are Expected To Be In The Future 61

What to do with the goals I have in mind? 64

Chapter Four: HR is Not Your Friend! 70

Things You Should To Never Share With HR 74

How to Bring An Issue To HR 78

Dangers Of Workplace Gossip And Harmful Criticism 80

Become a Confident and Grounded Worker 84

Chapter Five: Social Currency - The Importance of Finding Your Mentors, Sponsors, and Advisors 89

Who Are Mentors, Sponsors, and Advisors? 91

How to Win Over Mentors, Sponsors, and Advisors 95

Expanding Your Professional Network 101

Chapter Six: Do Not Pledge Allegiance to Cliques and Groups, But Also Don't Cut Them Off 109

Cliques vs. Teams 114

How to Recognize and Understand Your Office's Political Behavior 116

How to Deal With Cliques 120

Having Empathy vs. Suffering from Others' Pain 122

Strategies For Dealing With Office Gossip 124

Chapter Seven: Burnout Indicators 129

What Are Burn-Out Indicators? 133

The 5 Rules To Treat and Prevent Burnout 140

The Difference Between Self-Flagellation And Self-Compassion 142

How Can Self-Compassion Help You? 145

Stay True To Yourself 148

Chapter Eight: Failure Is A Temporary Friend 150

Renovation And Balance 151

Failure Isn't A Curse 152

The 10 Secrets Of Coping with Failure 155

Bouncing Back From Failure At Work 165

Chapter Nine: The Key To Train Yourself To Stay Positive 169

Cope With Negative Thinkers 173

Spread Positivity To Other People 176

The 38 Mental Ghosts That Sabotage Our Life Quality 177

Look At The Silver Lining 180

Practice Gratitude 181

Separate Fact From Fiction 182

Move More, Exercise More, And Improve Your Mood 186

Focus On Yourself 187

Chapter Ten: The Part To True Healing: Keep A Room For Better Days 189

The Importance Of Therapy 191

Why Should I Do Therapy If I'm Not the Problematic One at Work? 194

Getting Over Resentment 195

Searching For Therapists? 199

Cognitive Behavioral Therapy [CBT] 200

Conclusion **214**

Don't forget do DOWNLOAD your 28 Days Worksheet Journal Exercise **218**

Resources **219**

Introduction

Destructive and toxic behaviors, we experience them in our family, social circle, romantic relationships, and the workplace– they are everywhere. It's extremely important to know that the term "toxic people" may bring the idea that some person is broken or contaminated. When in fact, that person has behaviors that are harmful to the relationship with others. Meanwhile: they are not a lost cause. They have a full set of tools for changes to get a better understanding of how they treat others. The thing is... not everyone is willing to look inwards and try to work on themselves.

If you're reading this book, then like the old me, you're at a nerve-racking point in your life and need your sanity restored. Maybe you are unfortunate enough to be working with toxic individuals, being bullied at your workplace, or a victim of unfair politics from a department or coworker. The never changing fact is that working or interacting with people with toxic behaviors could be your worst experience.

Journey with me as I'll be sharing my results from deep research and personal experience on how to overcome toxic workplace relationships, office politics, and the emotional impact on our unconsciousness. I'm passionate about helping as many people as I can to overcome their toxic relationships and learn how to build healthier ones, and find closure to the old wounds that stop us from experiencing joy in the smallest things.

Workplace toxicity is more than having a bad day at work or not getting along with your colleagues. There are harmful acts that get in the way of your performance – I've been there. The toxic personalities make you feel psychologically distressed, physically exhausted, or mentally depleted.

Have you experienced this type of intense emotions at work? Or perhaps the description brings unpleasant memories of your personal experience with toxic people at work? Working with toxicity is never a pleasant experience because they tend to drain your productivity and ability to function well in the workplace, leaving you with feelings of fear, disgust, and lack of will.

People could have minor misunderstandings during a project or work interaction. Some people become a little pressured when in an important meeting or when they need to brainstorm with a coworker. However, when you are in a work environment with drainer coworkers, their presence fuels negative feelings that make you tired and insecure.

Look, this is what we need to bear in mind: Toxic coworkers aren't looking for ways to get better. They don't want to learn and benefit from the successes of others. All they need is someone on whom they can project their fears and hatred. They want to complain, nag, and spread exaggerated stories and lies around the workplace.

Besides being mentally unhealthy, toxic work relationships should not be endured or ignored. The insecurities caused by an intimidating boss or that annoying coworker should be addressed for your own sanity. You need to be conscious of your working environment to know the relationships that are destroying you since you spend a lot of time in your workplace and, over time, build relationships with colleagues, whether you like it or not.

The high level of workplace toxicity is fast becoming a norm since nothing is done to stop the narcissistic behaviors toxic people exhibit in a work environment. As management subtly turns a blind eye to these acts, you are not only dealing with toxic coworkers; you may have to endure the management or bosses that condone or perpetuate the same acts.

Of course, many of us have encountered different levels of workplace toxicity, including difficult bosses, controlling superiors, politics among groups, conflict rivalries, gossip, and annoying colleagues. However, not everyone is completely lucky or works in a perfect place.

I came into contact with a toxic work relationship at the tender age of 15. Growing up in a family filled with strong toxic traces, I needed an escape route. I needed something to take me from the house while earning a living. As a mid-teenage kid, I knew the odds were not in my favor, so I was already mentally prepared to face the pressure of the environment when I started working.

I had a goal I needed to achieve, so I gave my job everything as I diced in excitement. But the reality of things was different from the expectations I had in my head. Working in a toxic environment can be highly stressful and harmful. It could bring your self-esteem to the barest minimum or even damage your mental health – but I survived.

For several years, I was subject to conditions of the company and the behaviors of coworkers, and was forced to endure complicated office relationships and politics. Whenever I made a mistake, the narcissists became ecstatic! It didn't end there, I was yelled at, called different names, and I got paid a meager salary. Over time, I became demotivated due to the excessive negativity. It became difficult for me to socialize since I faced family members' toxicity when I returned to the only place I could call home.

It becomes even more complicated when you have to walk and work on eggshells at home and in your workplace – life will be almost impossible to be lived with joy.

If you're wondering how I survived and can remain sane enough to write about my experience with clarity and self-awareness, I would say it was due to the tiny light of hope I held on to, and also the resources I'm offering here in this book, especially to you, dear reader.

I once heard about different workplace conditions abroad (in the United Kingdom) and how the workers were treated respectfully. Workers are expected to work between 40 to 48 hours a week. If you make a mistake, you'll be called in separately and have a conversation. There were so many dream-like stories, and I wanted to go there and experience a better work environment, with more opportunities, and lead a better life. That was my GOAL.

To achieve my goal, as I learned how to deal with difficult people in my hometown, my skin got thicker over time. One of the ways to cope with workplace toxicity without breaking or losing focus is by learning how **to identify them, how they operate, and how to set boundaries**. You also need to learn when to speak out effectively against the abuse, hate, envy, oppression, and other forms of toxicity you experience in your workplace.

I remember not being much of an extrovert from my high school days. I'd rather sit in my room all day, listening to music, than step out for a party once in a while. Even when I was the different people I had to see daily.

So when I moved to the UK with my brother, I hoped things would be better, and we would conquer so many things together. It all started okay, and I was taking my time, trying to get the perfect job so I could settle in fully.

I got a job, and it started on a rough note. From the first day, the boss was demanding, and the workers were spiteful. Everyone seemed to have something against the other person. I was left in the middle, looking for whom to ask for advice and direction. But, everyone had nothing productive or mindful to say about the other coworkers, or even the tasks that we were supposed to do.

I had to figure it out myself. I wanted to preserve my sanity and still relate well with the different personalities in my workplace. So I had to do my best despite the constant disrespect and maltreatment. If you're like me, you probably already understand how that feels.

I know how tiring it is to balance your personal life and the tension in your workplace. Your boss is mean to you, and your coworkers don't do any better. They treat you like you don't deserve the job and make snide comments about your work ethic. They water down your achievements and make them look like nothing. I understand your pain, and I'm willing to help. I'll show you ways to get over the silly remarks from people in your workplace and focus on getting better at what you do.

We're bound to meet new people every day. Walking down to the grocery or exercising in the gym, we see many faces we've never seen before. These new faces don't bother us because they have nothing to do with our personal lives. Instead, our primary concern is with our family members and coworkers with whom we spend most of our lives.

After moving from Brazil to the UK to understand, know myself better, and find a more vital purpose in life, I realized that, just like me, many people have similar experiences, and even many more are looking for ways to break the cycle of a toxic environment and unhealthy workplace conditions. So I decided to write this book to help people by sharing great tools and resources to cope with these adversities in relationships.

I already have a book titled "Deal With Toxic Family Members", which you can find on Amazon, so we'll be focusing on dealing with coworkers in this book. It is a different approach, since the work environment requires a different posture when we encounter ourselves in front of people with not much intimacy as in our family. So this is definitely differently applied.

By the end of this book, you should've learned how to deal with different personalities at the workplace, understand healthy manners and how to act and react toward your coworkers and management alike. You should be inspired to pursue your goals without breaking under pressure and master how to change people's perceptions of you. Also, it's important to mention that all of these learnings should be applied with respect and integrity. The intention here is not to plant a seed of revenge or counterattack. **Nothing can be more disturbing against toxic behavior than an act of love and respect.**

Let's get started!

Chapter One: Working With Different Personalities

> *All too often, our personality is nothing more than psychological clothing that we wear to hide our true self from the world."*
>
> 
>
> *Teal Swan.*

It's shocking how much effect the people we work with have on our personal lives. For instance, if you have a supportive work environment, you're more likely to transfer your happiness with your family and friends. But, if you had a rough day at work, you'll go home feeling grumpy, with heavy energy too.

Being in a toxic work environment is incredibly challenging. It significantly impacts all facets of your life, including the quality of your job, your performance, and how you feel after work.

In my workplace, I experienced what I describe as having my energy sucked away. As a result, even after quitting the job where I experienced toxicity, I still had terrible ideas that affected my relationships and passions.

Real Meaning of "Surviving" In the Workplace?

I come from a family where every act seemed to choke me and make me feel uncomfortable. So, I naturally assumed that life would miraculously make my workplace a lesser burden to bear.

I thought burying my face in work all day would keep me distracted from the other troubles in my life. I was wrong! It turns out that life isn't a sea of roses. It has its challenges to make us grow up, and sometimes really fast! My workplace wasn't so different from what I experienced with some family members.

My workplace was a battle of ego and counterattacks. It was a lot to handle, because watching all of that bullshit going on around me, and having to pretend that I didn't know what someone said about someone else used to make me exhausted, with difficulty in trusting anyone there. Every day something new to observe and learn how not to act or react, from bosses that didn't think I was good enough to coworkers that thought I was doing too much for the position I was in the company. Nobody appreciated the effort I put in. It's as if it was strategically placed on, crushing my self-confidence and self-esteem.

I woke up every morning feeling angry that I had to face my manager and other coworkers. I would hold my breath and walk on eggshells throughout the day. I just hoped that I could find the north to start seeking. I needed to find a purpose for my life, and leave that environment, so I could breathe the light air of new experiences.

I wanted to quit, but then, I couldn't afford to. You probably have known this feeling at some point in your life, or that may be your current situation. When you have a family that depends on you, or you are with tons of bills to pay, or perhaps you don't have much money saved in your bank account. So it definitely didn't feel rational to quit my job just because I was not happy there, having to cope with the heavy environment. I decided to suck it up and survive it all with no deadline and expectations to change my situation.

If your perception of your surroundings is like mine at that moment, you probably have to "survive" in your workplace too. But are you surviving or shying away from all the problems that await you? Let's talk about it for a moment.

Surviving doesn't mean showing up tomorrow despite having a horrible day at work. It doesn't mean struggling to get a promotion or being stressed and overwhelmed to prove that you're good enough for the system you work in.

In reality, **surviving in the workplace means tackling years of emotional stress by reflecting on the past and taking steps towards recovery**. It means genuinely moving past bitter conflicts with coworkers, whether they hold executive, administrative, or other similar positions in the organization.

Conflicts in your workplace can take a tremendous toll on your confidence. You will feel like you're not good enough or your hard work isn't acknowledged. Surviving the workplace will teach you to change how you think about yourself so that other people will respect you too. It makes you think of getting better instead of dwelling on people's perceptions of you (and let's be honest here, we have no control at all about other people's thoughts, right?).

Most times, it's challenging to recognize the good side of things because you become immersed and obsessed with how things are going wrong for you. Surviving the workplace can help you look at the bright side. It helps you remember that you're the best at what you do and teaches you to let go of all hurts of the past and forge ahead.

The best thing to do is to observe how you spend your work day. Become conscious of how you choose to react to conflicts. If you discover you are uptight and rude because everyone else does it to you, you're not surviving the workplace. Instead, you're setting yourself to become negative and toxic as the other workers. Responding to them in the same language results negatively in more friction in the relationships.

How Do Coworkers Become Toxic?

We're so quick to criticize and judge others when we don't understand their pain. To fully understand why your coworkers act as they do, you need to be in their position and feel, or at least understand their pain.

The workplace is filled with different people, each with a unique temperament and personality. They're humans like you, so they also go through different issues and challenges. They've had different experiences and come from backgrounds you know nothing of.

Though each person in the organization has different functions, they all work for the same goal; the progress of the organization. The salary would serve as a motivator to keep the workers going. But the salary isn't enough motivation; human beings also love validation.

Imagine you are doing the same job with a colleague. You put in your best effort, but it just doesn't seem good enough. Yet, your colleague keeps getting congratulations and accolades daily for doing the exact same thing as you. How would you feel? Do you think you'll be sincerely happy for your colleague?

Human beings love being praised and appreciated for their good work. We want to stand out for being the ones with the best innovation or for putting in the most effort. Praise does something to our minds. It makes us feel valued and respected. It acknowledges our efforts and encourages us to do better.

If our efforts and accomplishments are not acknowledged, we may feel cheated or diminished. We start feeling unloved, unwanted, or irrelevant.

When workers feel irrelevant, they put in less effort and spite others who try to do better. The employee would also have feelings of self-doubt, insecurity, envy, and unhappiness. All these negative feelings begin to affect their work and rub off on other workers.

As social beings, we need to communicate on social and professional levels. We need to talk to others to help them share feelings of joy and pain. So, these aggrieved workers paint others badly to get support from other workers and employers. They portray other workers as being unkind, envious, and dishonest.

This is where the toxicity begins!

How Can You Spot Toxic Coworkers?

Who came to your mind when I was explaining how coworkers become toxic? If there's someone, that person might just be one of the workers in your workplace that needs special observation and care.

Toxic coworkers aren't looking for ways to get better. They don't want to learn and benefit from the successes of others. All they need is someone on whom they can project their fears and hatred. They want to complain, nag, and spread exaggerated stories and lies around the workplace.

They don't even know how to succeed in their personal lives, and they're not ready to learn. These folks will attempt to spread unflattering rumors, insults, or other negative remarks about others to you, and vice-versa.

When I think about it now, it's crazy that I couldn't recognize the warning signs of my colleagues' behavior and take action. Instead, I was drawn into their negative aura because I couldn't see them, even though they were there the entire time. Plus, I had this strong urge to please the people around me, afraid of conflicts or uncomfortable conversations.

Some coworkers are frequently complaining, exhaling a feeling that nothing and no one is good enough for them. The whining starts the minute they get into the office. The worst part is that they affect the ones around while complaining. It's a need to spread their negativity and get some moving head agreements to confirm their insecure affirmations.

They have no regard for the boundaries of other people. Instead, they extend their negativity to anyone, as for them, nobody is likable or trustworthy. They manage to use your words against you and assume that they're always right.

After speaking with toxic coworkers, you'll feel drained, discouraged, disturbed, or even humiliated. They can insult you and hurt your feelings by making sarcastic jokes. They would never say sorry and not listen to others because they believe they are the experts.

The secret behind it is... these coworkers battle with insecurity and self-doubt. This is why they get angry and feel triggered whenever others do great things. Because when they see others with joy and achieving things, this reminds them they don't feel capable of achieving great things too. When you somehow succeed, they will be envious of you and react to your success with sabotage, hostility, insults, and passive-aggressive behavior. They'll smirk and brag about themselves while encouraging you to tone it down and be 'average.' These people will do their best to find something to destabilize you.

Toxic coworkers are excited when you make a mistake and love seeing you suffer. If you try to ignore them or treat them in a similar way, they'll rant about how harsh and terrible you are. They're simply insatiable!

The Seven Personalities at Work

Sometimes, we wish everyone was just like us. We want every other person to think and react like us. We might even think others are toxic because they don't act as we do. But let's face it; there are different people and personalities worldwide. If we were all the same, life would be rather boring.

We often get irritated when we observe that others behave differently from us. But that's not right. You should make an effort to understand how your coworkers differ from you. It'll help you maintain a healthy and productive mindset.

Some people are more reserved and prefer to deliberate on their own. Others tend to be louder and yearn for social gatherings. Some are naturally born leaders, while others want to follow.

Now, let's have a look and discuss seven personalities you can find in your workplace.

1. ***The Driver***

You'll find this person settling disputes, encouraging team members, and keeping everyone on track. They also enjoy organizing and directing meetings and are skilled at delegating and handling emergencies.

The drivers in an organization usually have strong communication skills, a clear vision of projects, and the ability to inspire others. They also love leadership positions where they can make decisions independently, solve problems, and take calculated risks.

Drivers don't like dry, long, and pointless conversations. So, your discussions should have a focus or target. Keep it brief and straightforward.

2. ***The Influencer***

You can recognize influencers by their bubbly attitude and the desire to come together to work for everyone's good. They're diplomatic, ready to help, friendly, and open to making compromises.

Influencers appreciate teamwork and collaboration because they flourish in social environments. They also encourage others to be more imaginative and flexible.

You'll find them hanging out in the lunchroom or visiting people's desks during work hours. They enjoy social interaction and enjoy discussing current events or trending topics.

Most influencers aren't good at initiating plans, but you can count on them to complete tasks and resolve conflicts amicably.

Other personalities can also be good influencers. However, unlike other personality types, the influencers archetype prioritizes teamwork and success over personal gain.

When relating with influencers, it's best to adopt their style of friendliness and warmth. Always carry them along and make them feel loved because they cherish other people's approval.

3. The Supporter

The supporter is usually known for being calm and kind. Most workers in the organization love them because they're friendly and easy to work with.

They support others' ideas and act as a calming presence in difficult situations. They also complete jobs using low-risk or tried-and-true methods.

The strength of supporters is in their ability to establish solid, long-lasting relationships with others. They function best when provided with accurate and thorough information.

You must have the same peaceful vibe a supporter has to get along with them successfully. Give them regular reassurance or guidance because they, too, need to know they're doing their job well.

4. *The Analyst*

These kinds of coworkers are realistic. They prefer working independently rather than together.

Analysts get lost in their world of conceptualization and problem-solving. However, they have an eye for detail and can come up with original ideas and solutions that make the team's work stand out.

When working with an analyst, don't be overly casual or friendly. They'll react to what you say better if you stay on topic and are direct. Also, analysts love it when you give them structure and enough time to execute tasks.

5. *The Logician*

The logicians in your workplace are usually intelligent, inventive, and creative. They don't make decisions based on emotions and sentiments. Instead, they love to consider facts and figures before concluding.

Logicians have confidence in their ability to analyze complex situations and manage several projects simultaneously. However, they may appear insensitive or emotionless because of how they think and make decisions.

When you assign tasks to logicians, they prefer to be left alone with no supervision to figure things out themselves. They also love taking on difficult tasks to challenge themselves.

When working with a logician, please give them the liberty to solve problems independently. They'll also appreciate positive feedback and acknowledgment.

6. *The Campaigner*

Campaigners have a strong sense of self-motivation. Organizing events, participating in community service, and bringing order to the environment are things they enjoy doing. Campaigners have people skills but aren't people-pleasers. They would never prioritize popularity over a team project.

A campaigner would make an awesome mentor because they love encouraging people and want the best for others. They care deeply about helping others and can make someone's day better by just being enthusiastic.

To work well with a campaigner, you must be very calm and honest and give constructive criticism. Campaigners don't work well with pretentious or dishonest people.

7. *The High Achiever*

Most of your coworkers may fit this description. High achievers put forth great effort in whatever they do. They show consistency, reliability, and organization in getting their job done.

The high achievers are happiest and most productive when they're alone. They don't like starting conversations, and they like to operate in calm areas with no distractions. They put in a lot of effort and are incredibly innovative. Still, they lack social skills and the confidence to work in large groups. However, they function best in small groups where they feel more at ease sharing their ideas.

High achievers have good work ethics. They'll even go above and beyond the call of duty to do the job, even if it means coming in early and going home late.

Giving these kind coworkers more chances to develop and succeed is the best way to encourage them. They'll feel even more invested in their job and give you the respect you deserve.

Did you relate to one of these characteristics?

Keep Yourself Protected

It's important to know that different personalities will come across our path. But I wish someone had explained to me much earlier how to spot toxic behaviors and deal with them. Maintaining your positivity is a battle in an environment with a lot of negativity. So, you must learn to show empathy to toxic coworkers from afar. Being empathic doesn't mean putting yourself at the center of their complexities and joining their ideas, but making them feel visible and present, even with their harmful attitude. They will be seen with importance.

Trying to understand yourself is already difficult. So why add the drama of a toxic coworker to your list of problems? You don't have control over what other people do or think. So, just do you, but always respect them, despite their attitudes. It's important that you maintain a certain posture that shows them the boundaries you want to have.

It would be best if you also learned not to take things personally. It's okay to feel offended when someone ignores your opinions. However, don't take their actions too seriously. They act that way because of their problems and not just because of their personality. However, their attitudes say much more about themselves than about the victims they chose.

Dealing with toxic coworkers can be draining. It will affect your mood in so many ways. You must learn not to return the negative energy or cuss back at them. Instead, try to understand that their personality is different from yours. So, show them love and empathy from afar. In the long run, they'll give you the respect you truly deserve.

Knowing when the toxicity in your workplace becomes too much to handle is also very important. If you find that being in your workplace can result in serious mental issues like depression and anxiety, then it may be time to back off. Don't remain in a place that completely drains you emotionally.

Chapter Two: Changing People's Perception About You + 28 Days Workbook Journal Exercise

"Don't dwell on what went wrong. Instead, focus on what to do next. Spend your energies on moving forward toward finding the answer."

Denis Waitley.

How do we make others see us the way we do? Do you ever wonder what impression you have on your colleagues at work? Maybe you have been considered incompetent after failing to meet up with a deadine, or you've been tagged as a proud person after doing your job very well. How do you think you can change others' perceptions of you? Should you put more effort into changing your attitude, or should you just be yourself and be sure of your own values?

It can be quite annoying when people don't see you the way you want them to, but remember that you know yourself better than others. And your control over them is not with you.

People tend to read meaning into all of your actions. For example, when you decide to help someone fix their computer at work. Deep down, you just wanted to help or show kindness with no interest, second intentions, or negativity attached to it. However, others might feel that you are just trying to show off or get some benefit from it.

A person's perception may differ from what you feel is your truth. Still, sometimes their perception is not always necessarily wrong.

In this chapter, you will be exposed to various ideas you can consider while seeking to change how people see you at work. You can try several successfully proven exercises to restore your confidence about your best qualities. But first, let me quickly introduce you to Peter.

Meet Peter, a rising Product Manager for the Fortune 500 Company. Peter feels he is calm in how he talks, easy-going and friendly. Still, some of his colleagues and customers see him as talkative and a loser. Which perception do you think is correct? Does it really matter, trying to answer this question? Maybe it is not Peter's duty to be concerned with how they see him. Or maybe he should make some approach to their colleagues to talk about it, and clarify why they see him as they see.

A month later, Peter still sees himself as the best person to make deals but has recently gotten no deals or appointments. His customers are neither responding to his texts nor returning his calls. His colleagues also do not include him in important meetings. From this illustration, we can see that Peter needs to change how people view him.

We shouldn't rely on other workers' opinions, but setting a certain clarity of who you are, what your intentions are, and what your position is, can give coworkers a stable and transparent idea of you. Your qualities, your defects, your weaknesses, strengths, etc.

People's Perceptions of You at Work

But what are the things people can notice of my behavior? Below are examples of how people's perceptions of you at work operate.

- **Having the courage to speak up at the table**

Courageous conversations require verbal solutions to difficult problems like social justice, race, etc., to your colleagues at work. These conversations are called courageous because they involve the ability to be bold, brave, and confident in sharing your experiences and listening to other people's experiences as well, without getting into conflicts or fights.

Having these discussions challenges your point of view on matters. It also gives opportunities to discuss topics easily discarded.

Some people might think they are doing their best by overlooking things like skin color, gender, and social identities at work. Still, it's not healthy to overlook them since no one wants to be unnoticed. Acting like these issues don't exist leads to the continual existence of the problems.

When people are ready to eliminate their assumptions, and start connecting their ideas with others openly, it creates awareness about difficult experiences and clarity about the different perspectives. This also creates a healthy environment for working and makes employees more comfortable and connected with each other. Yes, being open to saying what you genuinely think with respect, obviously, creates a connection. When you decide to hide your opinion when you don't like something, instead of talking to the person involved, you build walls in the relationship.

Once I read in the book *Not Nice: Stop People Pleasing, Staying Silent, & Feeling Guilty... And Start Speaking Up, Saying No, Asking Boldly, And Unapologetically Being Yourself, written by Aziz Gazipura*, that partial communication creates partial connection. But full communication creates a full connection.

Certain conversations can be quite challenging at work when employees start to talk about the emotional aspects of their lives. However, it is essential to have them because it boosts the efficiency of workers when they are motivated and encouraged to bring their full selves to their work environment. Courageous conversations also increase trust and authenticity.

Having a courageous conversation about various triggers at work can be vital. Below are some ways to create an opportunity for courageous conversations.

o Recognize the atmosphere in the room.

Ask for the triggers in a conversation. When an incident happens, whether within or outside the workplace, it triggers the necessity to hold the conversation. Sadly, the workers might already have strong emotions about the topic.

You can create a small group seminar for your coworkers. Tell them that you are trying to create a safe space for them to talk about how they feel. You can mention feelings like anger, hatred, fear, or disgust in advance to avoid putting the first speaker in a tight spot.

- **Create a special time.**

Create awareness about the time and location of the meeting to assure your co-workers that the conversation will take place. You can do this by sending emails to them. Ensure you create enough time for each person to speak, which is why breaking them into smaller groups is important.

- **Create a model of what you wish to see.**

At the beginning of the seminar, put everybody in a single room, split them into fewer groups, and select leaders for each group. These leaders can create a platform for good communication. If you can remove fear from the workers by creating direct and open communication, it will help them share how they feel, and gain the willingness to be transparent.

Know that you can speak whenever you can at a table. Don't discard such an opportunity. Always believe that you are special and that your point of view or opinions matter. No judgment takes place in this moment, that's important to highlight.

○ Speaking their "language" to earn significance

Whenever you experience toxic behavior from your coworker, most times, you are expected to settle down your opinions and courage despite the aggressive attitude. Understanding ways to speak up for yourself with respect may surprise and overwhelm your toxic colleagues. Nevertheless, to be heard or stand up for yourself, you probably have to change how your voice sounds or speak a little more aggressively so that people can hear you. You may also have to pretend you accept others' opinions just to show how kind you are and to preserve the relationship.

Have you once pretended or even lied to people to gain significance or power within the company? If yes, then the toxicity may be influencing you greatly. You do not need to wonder or get confused about the approach you must take to handle your toxic colleagues.

If you feel some of your coworkers are draining your energy with their toxicity, here are some tips to keep the rumbling in check.

○ Know when the line has been crossed

The stage where you can healthily discharge toxic complaining may not come too soon. To be aware of the time you must vent off any toxic complaint healthily, you need to start tracking your feelings after facing a colleague whose complaints are getting on your nerves.

Start asking yourself how you feel when you walk away from a conversation. Notice what makes you feel weighed down whenever a colleague comes into your office. Is it that you do not feel excited to see them, or do they give some level of toxicity to you which has become unbearable? If that is the case, it is certainly the time to take action. Doing nothing about it can cause their negativity to overwhelm you.

To clarify, anytime your colleague yells at you, attempts to bully you, or displays extremely toxic behavior to you repeatedly. You need to address the issue. Such behaviors shouldn't be allowed in the work setting.

- **Set limits**

Having friends in the workplace is not bad, but know that everyone cannot be your friend. In your workplace, people can try to offload their baggage, especially when you want to work. It is fine to ask such colleagues to leave you alone. That is you being professional; you do not have to listen to everyone's deep dark stories or grouses in the workplace unless it has something to do with your job.

It is a good idea to shut your office doors, or if you have no doors, verbally inform your coworkers you are unavailable to chat during a few working hours. Placing workplace boundaries will help you by allowing you to focus on the most important thing - your work and trying to get it done. Once you achieve these, you can now open the door.

You can set your boundaries by saying, *"Hey, I will be glad to have a chat with you at the end of the day, but right now, I need to attend to work."* . You may also try using earphones to make yourself less approachable and turn off notifications to prevent digital distractions.

○ Bear in mind your colleague is human, too.

Toxic people live with lots of negativities in their inner or private life. Sometimes they tend to spill some of these negativities into the workplace. They might be suffering from depression, which causes them to see everything from a negative perspective. If you are comfortable reaching out to help such colleagues, then do so.

While you are not duty-bound to be their therapist, it might help you know what makes them display toxic attitudes. When you remember this and acknowledge that these experiences that people had have nothing to do with you, it can invoke some empathy and compassion. With that, you can give your colleague a little tolerance, and once you have listened to them based on your capacity, you can move on with your day.

However, you should not snub toxicity to the level where people feel okay to walk over you and speak up because they feel you will always respond or take responsibility. As stated earlier, there is nothing wrong with the desire to make everyone happy, but trying to achieve that can make you a wuss.

The 28 Days Worksheet Journal Exercise

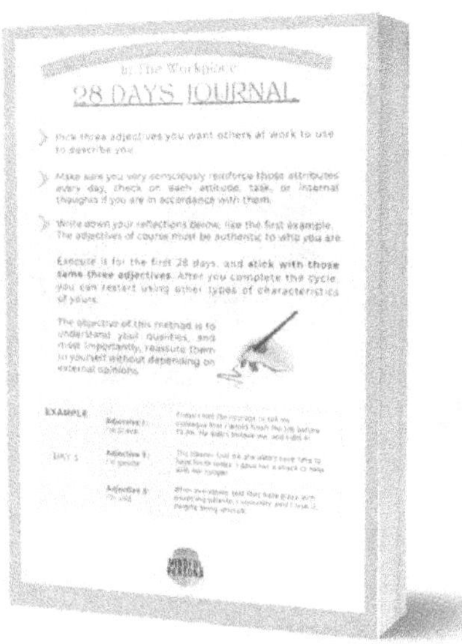

The objective of this method is to understand your qualities, and most importantly, reassure them to yourself without depending on external opinions.

If you'd like to **Download The 28 Days Worksheet Journal Exercise** at no cost at all, access it on my blog's home page:

www.mindfulpersona.com

Also, share your experience in our Private Facebook Support Group!

MP Therapeutic Writing Support Group

https://www.facebook.com/groups/mpwritingtherapy

This is a private group where you can write whatever makes you pleased, also learn, ask questions, discuss and get valuable content when it comes to improving Emotional and Mental Health.

Writing therapy, otherwise described in the literature as "expressive (emotional) disclosure", or "expressive writing", may have the potential to heal mentally and physically.

"I hear and I forget, I see and I remember, I write and I understand." - Proverb

This is a group you will get a lot from, which means you also should give and contribute to the community as well. We encourage you to share your experiences either with unsolved emotional struggles or wins, to inspire and help others with support. I hope to see you there!

How to Tell That Someone Needs Reassurance on The Job

When people need reassurance at work, it means they need someone to formalize their achievements. They want to hear people commending them for a job well done. Such people rely on reassurance at work to feel confident. Without validation, they will keep on doubting themselves and their abilities.

Colleagues in the workplace who need reassurance pose certain characteristics, and they include:

- Being unsure and self-conscious about their work performance.
- Always asking many questions just to be sure, even though they already know the answer to the questions.
- Often making statements that can be self-deprecating in a way to restore their confidence.
- Tend to reserve their opinions, keep out of any opportunity to volunteer, and continuously doubt themselves, even when they are right.

If any of these statements are pointing toward you, the 28 Days Exercise can help you and make your days productive, you can be sure of that.

You can tell that a workmate needs reassurance by their behavior. We all need some sort of reassurance in all aspects of our lives. However, the levels of assurance differ among people. So how do you work with someone who needs reassurance?

Training an Employee Who Requires Reassurance

If you are a boss in the workplace, assessing your employee's ideal level of positive feedback can help you do your work effectively and harness their potential for the better.

Here are two significant ways to train employees who need reassurance as a boss:

- Train showing your expression of approval or support, and be honest about how long it takes to understand different processes. This will help others stop worrying about everything they still don't know.

- Take note of how your colleague is progressing through training. You can achieve this by drawing up a training schedule or making a checklist, with the transparency that the employee needs to understand the big picture with you.

How You Can Motivate Your Workmate Who Needs Reassurance

- Think of various ways of rendering positive support so that you can naturally give feedback. Your colleagues can be reassured in many ways, and they will respond depending on the way(s) that resonates with them.

- Do not hold on to one way of giving positive feedback. In your workplace, there can be people that love to be recognized in front of their workmates, while some prefer to be called aside and hailed for their great job.

How To Give Feedback To Them

- Ensure you give positive and negative feedback accordingly during work. Someone who strongly desires reassurance may indeed get affected by negative feedback. However, if you let them see their mistakes and show them that the world will not end if they change, they will take the feedback as it is. You need to get your colleagues to trust that you will tell them the truth and what is needed for them to make a positive change or improve.

- If your coworker lacks self-confidence, and you can see it disrupting their work and progress, be honest with them about that. As you converse with them, you can instill confidence by letting them know when there is a problem that needs to be fixed. You should also avoid softening statements like "I think this might be a bad idea," or "This seems like a bad idea, but..." and so on. Instead, be direct and honest with what you say, and don't be afraid of instant reactions. They can happen in the first moment, as some people have different ways to digest what you say, interpret and understand it. This is a temporary feeling, and the best way to make things clear is through communication.

When your colleague gets frustrated, they may start experiencing some emotional meltdown. In chapter 7, you will be provided with tools to handle and overcome such challenges.

You have certainly learned a lot about changing people's views about you in your workplace. Well, it is not enough just to know; you need to start engaging in activities that allow you to be seen as the person you truly are in your workplace and help colleagues improve their attitude whenever you have a chance to.

What have you learned in this chapter?

- We discussed how to handle a courageous conversation with toxic colleagues in the workplace. We then expounded on ways to create an atmosphere to converse courageously.
- Next, we explained why and how it is necessary to speak the language or tone of toxic coworkers.
- After that, we provided a quality 28 days worksheet journal exercise that will help you prove your true self and build self-confidence.
- Finally, we talked about ways to observe if your colleague needs reassurance on their work.

There you have it! Let's head over to the next chapter!

Chapter Three: Goal Setting – Building a Foundation for A Better Future

> *If you do not know where you are going, you may end up anywhere, like you or not."*
>
> Lawrence J. Peter.

Humans are naturally subject to change. However, one might still wonder why we sometimes find it uncomfortable to change even when we know it is necessary to attain our goals. Fear holds us back, especially when it makes us uncomfortable.

You get to attract new opportunities when you make certain changes. Therefore, it would be best if you were open-minded to identifying and taking new opportunities. They can develop professional or personal skill sets necessary for creating a foundation for a happier and greater future.

Though you avoid changes naturally, you should aim to understand change better. Use your passion and purpose to keep yourself on track. Know that where you are today is not where you are going tomorrow. So if you have troubles at work that don't support your growth, start focusing on your goals and prioritize your mental health.

To start this chapter, here are a few questions for you to reflect on:

- What kind of person am I now?
- What person do I wish to become?
- What is my career goal?

Answering the questions can help you refresh your mind about what inspired you in the first place to take that first step. To remain consistent when things don't go as planned, don't be discouraged; instead, stay believing. Have faith that whatever you are experiencing, whether conflicts, frustrations, or struggles, they exist to build you up.

By the end of this chapter, you should be able to set your goals and know how to achieve them.

Understanding Long-Term Goals and Their Importance

Long-term goals refer to a significant height you aspire to achieve in your professional career within a long period, say 3 to 5 years. Of course, it could be longer for some people, depending on the career goal and the person.

Long-term goals help you to work with focus to attain that sought-after career goal in the future. You create a lucid picture of your expectations in your career path. It also shows you the skills you need to learn and things you need to experience to reach those objectives. Your goals, in most cases, may not be the same as your colleague. For example, you may be motivated by professional aspirations, while others may only aspire to attain some personal aim.

Do you desire a satisfactory and successful professional career? You cannot escape setting long-term career goals, and they are integral to achieving that desired height in your profession.

Furthermore, having long-term goals gives you something to exert effort for. It gives you a reason to struggle, a purpose. Maslow's hierarchy of needs throws more light on this matter. Maslow's hierarchy of needs in psychology is an inspirational theory that consists of 5 levels of the model for human needs. It is usually pictured as hierarchical grades within a pyramid.

The human needs listed from the bottom of the hierarchy to the top are:

The basic physiological needs include those that are vital to survival. In addition to the basic requirements of nutrition, air, and temperature regulation, it also includes shelter and clothing.

The security and safety needs are allocated at the second level of Maslow's hierarchy, the needs start to become a bit more complex. At this level, the needs for security and safety become primary. Finding a job, obtaining health insurance and health care, contributing money to a savings account, and moving to a safer neighborhood are all examples of actions motivated by security and safety needs.

Social needs include love, acceptance, and belonging. At this level, the need for emotional relationships drives human behavior. In order to avoid loneliness, depression, and anxiety, it is important for people to feel loved and accepted by others. Personal relationships with friends, family, and lovers play an important role, as does involvement in groups—such as religious groups, sports teams, book clubs, and other group activities.

The Esteem level has a need for appreciation and respect. At this level, it becomes increasingly important to gain the respect and appreciation of others. People have a need to accomplish things, then have their efforts recognized. People need to sense that they are valued by others and feel that they are making a contribution to the world. Participation in professional activities, academic accomplishments, athletic or team participation, and personal hobbies can all play a role in fulfilling esteem needs.

Self-Actualization represents self-awareness, the ones concerned with personal growth, less concerned with the opinions of others, and interested in fulfilling their potential. Maslow's said of self-actualization: "It may be loosely described as the full use and exploitation of talents, capabilities, potentialities, etc. Such people seem to be fulfilling themselves and doing the best that they are capable of doing. They are people who have developed or are developing to the full stature of which they are capable."

Before dealing with the needs higher up in the hierarchy, the needs at the bottom must be first attended to.

Self-actualization
desire to become the most that one can be

Esteem
respect, self-esteem, status, recognition, strength, freedom

Love and belonging
friendship, intimacy, family, sense of connection

Safety needs
personal security, employment, resources, health, property

Physiological needs
air, water, food, shelter, sleep, clothing, reproduction

We can know more and understand better the importance of setting long-term goals through Maslow's pyramid. Here are some qualities associated with defining long-term career goals.

➢ **Motivation**

It has been found that the more people strive toward self-actualization, the more they are inspired, and their level of effectiveness improves. In other words, as you recognize what you can do, your capability, and what you can or cannot handle, you tend to be highly motivated to keep striving toward self-actualization.

When you set long-term goals and achieve them, you will be inspired even to attain greater levels. It is an instinctive reaction to the non-stop improvement seeking.

➢ Personal and Career Growth

No one wants to remain stagnant in their professional and personal growth. As an individual, your needs are complicated, you want to be happy with what you do, and you want to take pride in the things you have accomplished. In addition, you desire to be respected in the work environment. However, attaining them without working on a long-term professional strategy is impossible.

➢ Fulfillment

Maslow claims that fulfillment does not seem the same for different individuals. Each person has their way of defining their objectives, which are defined according to what the person feels is most necessary. For instance, you may define fulfillment as being able to earn a particular amount as a salary. In contrast, others may view fulfillment as attaining the highest level in their specific profession.

When you set long-term career goals for yourself, you most likely feel fulfilled when you reach that goal, that's the main point here. Actually, there is a saying that states that happiness is not in the end result of your goal, but during the path you take to it.

➢ Extra Flexibility

One reason people seek long-term career goals is that it usually renders jobs with flexibility. The Covid-19 pandemic expressed how important jobs with flexibility are to employees. In that period, parents with such jobs had to work from home, and they could care for their children as they worked. Other employees with such flexible jobs did not need to risk their health but remained indoors to work.

Organizations or firms that render these jobs, mostly higher workers, have engaged in a long-term career pursuit. This means that long-term goals can bring job security.

➢ Social Interaction

Apart from the need for a flexible job, the Covid-19 pandemic has exposed why it is necessary for people to stay connected to each other. A flexible workplace helps people spend more time building up necessary relationships instead of working and having to travel.

➢ Healthy Work/Life Balance

Most of us understand how much the balance between our work and the rest of our lives is being hit hard by having to commute to the workplace early in the morning and return in the evening.

Can you relate it with the time of the pandemic, when people just worked from the comfort of their homes? You excel in your profession because you are committed to a long-term goal, but that does not mean you should sacrifice other aspects of your life. Other aspects of your life are as important as your work life and should not be overlooked. However, you must be concerned if your work/life is not balanced enough.

You can rearrange the pattern of your life and reconstruct your long-term objectives to attain a balance that makes you feel better.

Recognizing Where You Are Currently On Your Career Path And Where You Are Expected To Be In The Future

Do you know how far you have gone in your long-term goal pursuit? How much ground have you covered? How much ground is left to cover?

If you do not know how to answer these questions, then this section of the chapter is mostly for you. However, an individual who knows his/her current position and future expectations can easily draft out the steps to take to get there.

We experience significant changes in our lives over a year, and most of those changes are not expected. Yet, we are compelled to adapt to the changes affecting our work and lives. Unfortunately, this change causes many to doubt the possibility of achieving their goals and assigning priority to them.

You may agree with me that it can be very confusing and obscure when you decide to set long-term career goals. For instance, new university graduates mostly do not know what they would like to do, their abilities, and the kind of skills they want to learn. So they stay confused, and this confusion can last for a whole year after graduation, something which would have been sorted out by creating long-term career goals. But, unfortunately, most of us, just like these graduates, delay a lot in deciding our long-term career goals.

It shows how setting long-term career goals can be very critical. It would help if you planned your path to your goal so that your future expectation will be certain. In addition, you will be able to pursue a career goal that will bring you great contentment.

Are you still in the place of trying to know what your long-term career is and what your path should be like? I have put together a model for setting SMART goals. In addition, I have mentioned good examples of goals you might desire to go after.

The acronym "**SMART"** is the key to setting career goals that you can achieve.

S

SPECIFIC - State specifically what you desire. For instance, saying that you want your books to hit more sales this year is not the same as saying that you want your books to hit 1000 sales this year. When you are specific about your goals, the tendency to achieve them is high.

M

MEASURABLE - Career goal settings require clarity on how you will quantify your achievement. For example, if you want more of your books to be sold, how much more? If you want to connect more people to your marketing business, then state how many.

A

ADJUSTABLE - Ensure that your career goals are flexible enough. We can predict the future, but things may not go as planned; that is how life works. It does not matter how well you plan your career goals. You ought to adjust them both size-wise and time-wise.

R

REALISTIC - When you set your long-term career goals, make sure they are realistic or achievable at the specified time. The more you set goals and next steps to follow, less you want to discourage yourself when you fail. Aiming to be like the CEO of Tesla -Elon musk, is a good thing, but the path to attaining that must be fully set.

TIMELY - A great and possible long-term career goal must be timely. For example, you do not have to travel to the United States for Dan Lok's one-week lectures on how to earn more than 1000 boxes a day in copywriting when you are still a first-timer and need several weeks to learn.

What to do with the goals I have in mind?

➢ Write Them Down

Suppose you are the type that pictures your long-term goals in your mind but leaves them in your memory. It may start to become indistinct and unclear. It is best practice to put them down on paper. It is said that the faintest pencil retains information more than the best human memory.

➢ Visualize Them

You can sketch out your goals or create a simple inspirational poster and post it somewhere you can always look at daily, like your wall, desk, or even in the wallpaper background of your phone screen.

➢ Start Small

You might feel intimidated when trying to set huge career goals for yourself. You can also get disheartened, especially when you do not know where to begin. Therefore, split your objectives into smaller steps, and begin with something very small daily. You will be highly encouraged if you consistently accomplish a tiny part of your goals daily.

Consistency is the key to long-term goals. If you can make every day a little bit, you will get there, eventually, before you even expect it. Some say that making your bed is the first step of your day, so you send a message to your brain that your daily tasks start being done with the simplest thing. Then, you tend to think of what is your next move.

➢ Tell Others About Them

When you let others know your long-term career objectives, they can help you to stay focused on them. It creates life for your visualization. They can remind you of your resolutions towards achieving them. Of course, it could go the other way around, and they will try to discourage you, but this is where you must be resilient and remain unchanged about your goals.

Some people normally say, "don't share your plans until you make it, so nobody will screw them." Actually, this superstition is terribly limiting. Once you don't share, you don't get ideas, opinions, bits of advice, or even constructive criticism from other people. These things are helpful if you know what to absorb and what not to.

➢ Answer The Question "What Next?"

What is the next thing to do when you must have attained that desired height in your career? What will you do after making 1000 sales of the ebook within a year? What will be your next step? There's got to be something even greater than your long-term goal.

If you sincerely do not know what to do next, then your goal setting is not yet complete. You must draw a more elaborate plan that answers the question, "what comes next?"

Here are a few examples of long-term professional goals you can have.

- Maximize your earning potential or earn a promotion
- Land your dream job/business
- Develop new job skills
- Expand your professional network and gain global experience

Unfortunately, there are many alternative long-term career goals, all of which cannot be contained in this book. Ensure you do some personal research if you are interested in setting a new career goal.

Unfortunately, so many people still wallow in ignorance and resistance to change. Still, that number has just reduced, as I know you will make conscious efforts to be different. So get up now and grab a pen and a paper, write down your goals and make calculative plans to attain your long-term goals.

In this chapter, we were able to cover:

- Availing yourself for change.

- Understanding long-term career goals and knowing their importance.
- Knowing how to set attainable but exceptional career goals with the SMART technique.
- How to develop long-term goals and know the next steps after accomplishing long-term career goals.

Don't forget to make the most of this information. See you in the next chapter!

Chapter Four: HR is Not Your Friend!

Do not see your team's HR representative as a friend. It's easy to see them as one — they're right there, they are a people person, and they will listen. But, simply put, HR is not your friend."

Chris Williams.

The first human resources departments were created in the 1900s because companies tried to maximize employee performance by putting compensation systems in place. The companies then cared about keeping employees happy since no one wanted their staff to unionize. HR was the middleman between the workers and those at the company's top. HR told the boss, "Hey, look, the staff are unhappy about this or that." They became an avenue for staff to air their grievances to the higher-ups.

Eventually, HR departments became an advocate for employees, but this was only true until the 1970s. Once the threat of unionization started to decline in the 1980s, companies no longer cared about what their workers wanted.

At this point, companies just wanted to stay out of trouble with the government, thanks to all the worker protection laws being put in place. So, HR's advocacy shifted from the workers to the company. It was all about how to help the company comply with the new laws.

Now, while the new mandate was for HR to protect the company, this sometimes aligned with employee protection – like if an employee was harassed or discriminated against by their supervisor or manager. In this case, HR worked to prevent potential lawsuits against the firm.

The Role Of HR In The Workplace

It is the responsibility of Human Resources to carefully balance employees and company needs while ensuring that none interferes with the other. But when push comes to shove, HR will always choose the company. Their ultimate responsibility is to the firm, not you or your coworkers. Therefore, HR isn't your friend.

When your workplace is a toxic environment, it's normal to want to go to HR first. Perhaps your manager is discriminating against you in whatever way. Your first instinct is to report to HR – after all, they're there for employee protection.

However, finding out that complaining to HR won't always produce a positive outcome can be a rude awakening. It won't produce a good outcome for most companies. Obviously, there are still companies that have a more delicate approach to the employee, but the big majority work under these conditions.

While you shouldn't think of HR as an advocate for you or your coworkers, you should still have some clear expectations of them. You cannot always trust HR to do what is best for employees, especially if you're familiar with or you've had a similar experience to that of Susan Fowler and Uber.

According to a 2017 Society for Human Resource Management survey, only 33% of employees are satisfied with the relationship between employees and management. Another 2018 survey of the top tech firms in the US found that over 70% of employees at the Big Four firms (Apple, Amazon, Google, and Microsoft) didn't trust the HR departments. You'd agree that these are awfully low numbers, suggesting that trust is not prominent in employee-management relationships.

One mistake employees often make thinking that HR is in place to be their career coach. Nothing could be more wrong. And if you're one of those with this mindset, you might want to do away with it now.

You might be tempted to go to HR to report and discuss issues with your coworkers or manager. This seems reasonable, but whenever you bring a complaint or grievance to HR, they document it permanently on your employee record. HR marks you as having an issue. What does this mean?

It means that HR views you as someone who can potentially disrupt the workplace harmony they're paid to keep in check. It would be best to never go to HR unless you're confident you can present your case properly and fully understand your action's potential consequences. The key is setting boundaries and knowing what you should and shouldn't bring to human resources.

Things You Should To Never Share With HR

Before you bring a secret about yourself or your career to the HR department in your firm, be aware of how your employer might perceive the situation. In that light, here are eight things to never share with HR.

1. Leaving During A Leave

Whether you're on medical leave, taking care of a sick relative, or just welcoming a newborn baby into your home, it's natural to think about leaving work –

especially if you believe not going back would be best for a lifestyle balance. But even if you have this thought, it isn't something to share with human resources.

Doing so might leave your employer in doubt of your commitment or reliability. And if you decide not to leave, it can affect your reception when you return to work. Even if your employee can't legally fire you while on leave, they could demote or transfer you to a less prestigious department. So be sure to give HR the correct and assertive information.

2. Lying For Leave Extensions

Sometimes, employees invent lies and excuses to get extended leaves from HR. Unfortunately, lying for leave extensions isn't something everyone gets away with. If you lie, it can come back to haunt you, particularly if you genuinely need time off. In most cases, your employee can terminate you for lying about needing leave extensions. Remember that HR documents everything you bring to them.

3. Changes In A Partner's Career

Possible changes in your partner's career are something you absolutely shouldn't bring to HR until it is certain. You need to speak to your employer if you know the change will require you to reduce work hours, move to a new city, or get a new job – but don't bring it up at work until it's finalized. Otherwise, it can make you ineligible for certain benefits.

4. Moonlighting

If you have full-time employment at your workplace and still have a second job, that's not something to tell the HR department. What moonlighting communicates to human resources is that you aren't fully committed to your current job, which makes you seem unreliable. Your employer might blame failings such as late arrivals, delayed work, or unavailability for meetings on your second job. They can use this as a ground for firing or denying you compensation.

5. Lawsuits Against Former Employers

If you've ever filed a lawsuit against a former employer, that's not something you want to mention to your current one. Even the most ethical human resources departments live in constant fear of lawsuits. Sharing information about previous lawsuits at your new job can put you under threat watch. Suppose you're hunting for a new job. In that case, you should know that employers discriminate against those with lawsuits against former employers secretly.

6. Information About Your Health

You shouldn't share information about health concerns until they start to affect your performance at work. Otherwise, you risk boxing yourself out of opportunities, promotions, transfers, and leadership positions.

Making your employer privy to health issues can make them work around you to protect productivity and profitability. If you need to take a medical leave, it's best to speak to HR but wait until it becomes inevitable.

7. Personal Issues

Personal troubles don't belong at work – you shouldn't share them with HR or coworkers unless it's someone you have a good interpersonal relationship with. Bringing personal issues to work can directly or indirectly affect opportunities at work, create a bias against you, or make you seem unnecessarily difficult and unreliable.

However, if something from your personal life threatens to spill over into the workplace, you can share this information with human resources. At the same time, don't arm your employer with any information that doesn't contribute to or affect their goal of a team-oriented work environment.

8. Prohibited Activities

Activities that go against a company's policy, such as recreational drug use, shouldn't be discussed in the workplace. It doesn't matter if you engage in these activities outside work or during office hours. Human resources may be compelled to report you to law enforcement agencies regardless of where or when you do that prohibited activity.

If you've had criminal charges brought against you in the past, sharing this with your employer can make them deem you untrustworthy. Personal business should remain private unless it threatens to spill over into work.

However, let's say you applied for a new job with a felony on your record. In that case, you should reveal it if asked in your application.

How to Bring An Issue To HR

If you believe that you've been wronged at work and you have no choice but to bring the matter before HR, there are steps you can take to protect yourself appropriately. First, speak to someone outside of work with an extensive background in human resources. Ensure you do this before filing a complaint or drafting a letter detailing your experience or the situation.

This person can prepare you by asking all the questions you'll be asked by your HR department and guide you on how to answer each question correctly. Getting prepped by a professional can help you avoid saying the wrong things.

Bringing an issue before HR is similar to having a court case. You might say the wrong things without adequate preparation, which inevitably affects your credibility. Even worse, you might look like a troublemaker who wants to disrupt workplace harmony for no good reason.

Fear is the one thing that stops employees from filing claims with HR. Depending on the issue's seriousness, going to HR can jeopardize your job and livelihood. So, before you go, ensure you aren't in a position where that job is your only option.

You can boost your confidence and ability to move on from that toxic work environment by keeping references in check, tuning up your resume, mobilizing your network, and creating a list of potential employees you'd like to work for. This also helps if the company decides that the best course of action is to terminate your employment.

Again, you mustn't bring a grievance to HR unless it's something you cannot overlook. I will be honest; if your grievance is bad enough to bring to human resources, you most likely won't be working in that company long-term.

The best choice for you personally and professionally may be to move on to a new employer where you won't find yourself constantly reminded of the toxic situation. However, if the situation isn't that bad, you can find a way to work among these toxic energy vampires and feel good about yourself.

Before we talk about how you can cope effectively in a toxic work environment, let's briefly discuss the dangers of workplace gossip.

Dangers Of Workplace Gossip And Harmful Criticism

The workplace can be a hub of gossip, but at no point do you want to be at the center of it. Ordinarily, criticism, verbal warnings, and gossip in the workplace shouldn't hold you back. You should see them as a tool for personal improvement and maturity and enhancing your work experience.

Unfortunately, workplace gossip can have a serious impact if the other person has significant power over you. If you somehow find yourself in the middle of malicious backstabbing by your coworkers or boss, you must take an emotionally intelligent approach to deal with the issue.

Contrary to what you might think, your success in the workplace isn't a direct result of how other people evaluate you. You're the only one capable of ensuring your success by establishing value, achieving goals, and proving your worth.

Some of the negative consequences of uncontrolled workplace gossip for both employees and employers are:

- Wasted time and decreased productivity
- No trust and low morale
- Attrition when effective employees leave the company due to an unhealthy work environment
- Destroyed reputations and hurt feelings
- Increased anxiety since there'll be rumors as a result of no clear explanation of what's true
- Division among employees as everyone

There's nothing mean-spirited coworkers want more than **seeing you react to their slander**. They derive joy from seeing you hurt and miserable, so don't give them something to celebrate. Go into work with determination and indifference. More importantly, let your boss see your dedication to work.

Secondly, **do not retreat**, be it physically or emotionally. Despite how bad the situation may seem, you should have a few steadfast friends at work. You can share your work problems with your support network, who will remind you of how valued you are. And wear this as a protective armor every day you walk into work.

Remind yourself of all the reasons why **you're valuable**. Affirming yourself can reinforce your self-esteem, making it even easier to deal with criticism. Even if you have to write sticky notes or send texts to yourself, you'll find that self-affirmation can make a huge difference in how you feel while working in a toxic workplace with toxic coworkers.

Do not retaliate. It's the worst thing you can do, especially if the gossipmonger has significant power over you in the workplace. Stooping to your bully's level will only perpetuate the drama and mess.

Maintain eye contact, speak in a level and calm tone, and excuse yourself from the conversation. If any bullies are confident enough to say things to your face, be careful not to give in to the temptation. Please don't say or do anything they can use against you or spread behind your back.

Not only will the malicious person walk away with nothing, but you will have scored a major emotional and personal victory. The thing about coworkers with malicious intent is that they have a problem that has nothing to do with you.

The best way to deal with workplace bullies is to **ignore them**. So long as you don't give them the satisfaction of seeing you hurt, the bullying can't last. They'll move on to someone else as soon as they find out they can't take out their anger on you.

Sadly, this knowledge has given birth to the rise of toxicity in the workplace. Even though most companies have formal policies regarding gossip, criticism, and harm, toxic coworkers tend to band together. That can make it difficult for the company to implement policies. Don't be surprised if management takes the side of workplace narcissists and bullies.

The best way to deal with workplace narcissists, bullies, energy drainers, and generally toxic people is to become a more confident and grounded version of yourself. You are your best chance at handling everything toxic people throw your way in the workplace.

Become a Confident and Grounded Worker

A toxic work environment can create self-doubt and insecurity even in the most self-assured person. But with the tips I'm about to share, you can protect yourself from overthinking and become more confident and grounded.

It's normal if you sometimes lack confidence – truly confident people are also insecure on some level. If someone claims to be confident and self-assured at all times, they most likely aren't confident. There's nothing wrong with feeling uncertain sometimes, criticism or not.

The first thing to know about confidence is that it isn't overt, brash, or bold. Unlike what many think, confidence is a quiet and subtle expression of ability, expertise, and self-worth. The following are qualities you can cultivate to improve self-confidence.

➢ ***Don't be afraid of being wrong***

Be secure enough in yourself to admit when you don't have all the answers. Confident people don't take a stand because they think they're always right. No, they do because they aren't afraid of being wrong. If you want to convey confidence in the workplace, you must let go of the idea that you must always be right. You'll only come across as a bully if you don't.

➢ ***Listen before you speak***

Confidence requires you to be quiet and unassuming. Do not brag – insightful people can see that it's a facade to mask insecurity. Try to listen more times than you speak. Talk to your coworkers about what they do, how they do it, what you like about their work, and what you learn from them. The only way to learn from others is to listen more than you speak.

➢ *Duck the spotlight*

Don't try to get all the glory. Perhaps you did the bulk of the work in your team. Maybe the team overcame some major obstacles due to your hard work. A truly confident person doesn't need to ask for the spotlight – they may even actively avoid it.

Even if you care, don't seek validation from others. As I said earlier, what people think of you doesn't directly affect your abilities. What matters is your self-perception because true validation comes from within.

Don't be afraid to stand back and celebrate your accomplishments through your team members. If you step from the spotlight and let others shine, it will be a massive confidence boost for everyone on the team.

➢ *Ask for help freely*

Some believe asking for help signifies weakness, particularly in a competitive workplace. That couldn't be further from the truth. While asking for help does imply a lack of knowledge, experience, or skill, truly confident people are secure enough to admit strengths and weaknesses. So, they have no problem seeking help from others.

Not only does asking your coworkers for help mean that you're secure enough to admit when you need assistance, but it's also an opportunity to pay a huge compliment to the other person. It means you trust and respect their ability, skill, and expertise.

➢ ***Own your mistakes***

Confidence is marked by sincerity and honesty. You must be willing to own your mistakes to become more confident and grounded. When you reach a place of true confidence, you'll have no problem with 'looking bad.' People don't laugh at genuine and unpretentious people – they laugh with them. A lack of confidence can breed artificiality, which isn't a quality of a grounded worker.

Finally, being a more confident and grounded worker means you'll only seek the approval of those who matter. Nothing beats earning the trust and respect of a few people who truly matter in your personal and professional life.

No matter what you do or what decision you make, as long as you have a strong social currency and the support of those who truly matter, you'll be able to do it with true confidence.

In the next chapter, we'll discuss how you can build a strong social currency in and out of the workplace.

Chapter Five: Social Currency - The Importance of Finding Your Mentors, Sponsors, and Advisors

> *A mentor empowers a person to see a possible future and believe it can be obtained."*
>
> Shawn Hitchcock.

Ask anyone how they got to the level they are in their career, and you'll quickly learn that having a strong professional network is the single, most important thing you can do for your career. Talk to different successful people, and you'll find a few recurring themes: passion, strong performance, and an excellent work ethic.

Press a little further and ask what's the difference between these people and those who had similar qualities but never peaked professionally. You'll hear one thing: a strong social network of people who believed in them and were willing to help them climb the ranks. In other words, mentors, sponsors, and advisors.

Many of the successful professionals you see have connections. It's important to state that these people didn't have their connections handed to them. They had to forge them through professional networking.

There's only so much you can do for yourself in the workplace or any other professional setting. Career progression in a company or within the industry you find yourself in is driven by vital relationships that you must build from scratch.

Work, in general, revolves around people. Therefore, success in the workplace is driven, in part, by your relationship with people, especially those within your professional circle. It's critical for everyone to build and maintain real professional connections. This is especially important if you have major career and professional goals.

The Need To Build Your Social Currency

Building your social currency in the workplace requires initiative. You must be willing to put effort into meeting people, establishing a relationship, and subsequently maintaining it.

Networking is a deliberate and purposeful activity. You do it to establish, reinforce, and maintain mutually-beneficial relationships with people that can further your professional goals within and outside your industry.

In many countries, having a mentor isn't as commonplace as in the US or the UK. So, you might not be fully familiar with the concept unless you live or work in the West.

Earlier, I mentioned that a professional network should comprise mentors, sponsors, and advisors. Few people know the differences between all three, but that knowledge is crucial. Having these resources in your life can make a massive impact at different points and for varying reasons.

Most professionals only talk about having a mentor, which means they don't know what a sponsor does differs from what mentors and advisors do. That obstructs them from setting the right expectations or achieving desired results.

Who Are Mentors, Sponsors, and Advisors?

Mentors, sponsors, and advisors are relationships you should use to learn. They offer an opportunity to form partnerships with people with more knowledge and experience than you about different aspects of your career that you might want to explore.

Before I proceed, let's look at the distinct definition of each professional relationship.

➢ Mentor

This individual shares tips, resources, and vital information with their mentee. A mentor also offers motivation and emotional support when necessary. They could be someone within or outside your company, a friend, or someone aware of your professional context who can offer advice tailored to you and your goals.

Your mentor should be someone who can double as your role model. Because of this, you should be willing to trust them with the good, the bad, and the ugly – trust your mentor to be discreet about whatever information you share.

That is important because you want your mentor to be someone you can share details of what's working and what isn't in your life. They may even be familiar with happenings in your personal life, to an extent. Most importantly, you should be able to ask them for help on how to resolve your problems.

Every time you speak to your mentor should be seized as an opportunity to set goals, explore career options, identify resources, and highlight tasks to complete.

➢ Sponsor

A sponsor throws their weight behind you, your company, or professional events through material incentives. I would say that the sponsor is the one important relationship to cultivate among all three. Unfortunately, the concept of sponsorship isn't as commonplace as it should be. Thus, finding a sponsor remains elusive to many professionals.

Sponsors are strong advocates in powerful and influential positions. They are capable of providing life-changing opportunities or lobbying on your behalf. A sponsor is someone capable of pounding the table for you behind closed doors. And they're willing to protect you when you take risks. In contrast, mentors provide career guidance but don't necessarily have the power or influence to change your career trajectory.

Getting a mentor is much easier than getting a sponsor. In many cases, you can find your mentor via structured company programs. You can't find a sponsor based on merit or desire. Simply meeting someone and asking them to be your sponsor won't cut it. This isn't a relationship you can engineer through a standard matching, which explains why most companies don't bother trying.

Unlike a mentor, a sponsor is someone you only tell the good and the good – they shouldn't know about the bad and the ugly. The reason for this is that your sponsor is the person who will support you passionately in meetings and places you may not even have access to.

➢ Advisor

An advisor is a person who gives professional or career advice that can help you achieve your goals by helping to create short-term and long-term goals. You want your advisors to be people who are resourceful enough to help you formulate and evaluate plans, initiate projects, and assess progress. They should have specific experiences and multidisciplinary expertise.

Your advisor can also offer you guidance and review your goals and objectives. And as I mentioned before, review your progress towards set goals. Depending on the kind of network you're trying to build, and what you want to achieve, it's okay to have different advisors about different aspects of your career. Each advisor can act as a consultant in a specific area.

How to Win Over Mentors, Sponsors, and Advisors

Unless you're born with privileges, winning over people who can help your professional career is one of the hardest things you'll ever have to do. Although everyone knows that networking is a critical factor toward professional success, people don't realize how often they should make an effort to build and expand their network.

Suppose you've been in your field or industry for a few years. In that case, you probably already have a network. However, finding mentors, sponsors, and advisors can be difficult if you aren't good at networking.

Just thinking about where to begin can overwhelm you initially, but don't think of networking opportunities with fear or anxiety. Instead, view them as opportunities to advance your career. You'll get the hang of it in no time, and you may even surprise yourself.

Socialize With People

The first step to winning over mentors, sponsors, and advisors is to learn how to socialize with people inside and outside your firm. Getting to know your coworkers and establishing deeper connections is key to job fulfillment. At the same time, socializing at work requires you to maintain a standard of professionalism. Finding the balance between being professional and building relationships that are more than just 'work' is the essence of learning to socialize.

First, you must participate in social engagements for work, such as corporate or industry events, small gatherings of professional colleagues, and team-bonding activities. Every social event is an opportunity to engage colleagues in a structured setting.

These environments allow you to facilitate conversations with potential mentors, sponsors, advisors, and anyone who could be a part of your professional network.

Build A Positive Perception

Perception is everything in professional settings. So, steer clear of office gossip and cliques. You do not want to engage in activities that may affect or damage your relationship with potential mentors or sponsors.

While trying to socialize, it's normal to encounter different workplace cliques. These are colleagues who band together based on shared interests and keep other coworkers away from their group. Often, these cliques engage in gossip, bullying, and other negative behaviors that create drama in the workplace.

You must maintain a respectful and positive relationship with most of your coworkers. Avoid participating in this behavior because it limits your network. Also, be as inclusive as possible in your networking attempts.

Engage with everyone, including those you share interests with and people with different perspectives. Your professional colleagues will appreciate your charisma and kindness. Additionally, inclusive socializing makes you a team-oriented person interested in building a diverse professional network. That makes you much more attractive to potential mentors and sponsors in your workplace.

Showcase Your Expertise

This could mean being a thought leader, a content leader, the best person in your field, or a uniquely positioned innovator. Industry or sector notwithstanding, sponsors seek out those who offer unique knowledge or capability. They want someone whom people universally agree on their mastery level. If anyone could win over sponsors, everyone would have a sponsor.

For someone to accept to be your sponsor, they have to believe that you're the best at what you do. Nobody will throw their weight behind someone who won't make them proud of that decision – that's the cold, hard reality.

Be Indispensable

We can't be replaceable, but we can for sure be indispensable. This approach involves taking the initiative to help senior leaders in the company. For example, you could fill work gaps or execute a big project. Usually, a sponsor identifies work gaps themselves, but you can make yourself indispensable by identifying them before they do.

With this approach, you must go above and beyond your official role and even take on extra tasks and assignments. The good thing is that your efforts will all be worth it because doing that inspires deep loyalty from your sponsor – especially since you provide them with great leverage.

With this approach, you don't need to be the expert or the thought leader. It only requires you to be proactive and willing to take on more. When you step in to fill a void (with or without prompting), you display attentiveness, leadership, and drive – things that are more important to many sponsors than showing expertise.

And you don't necessarily have to impress the top executives at work; the key is to catch the eye of an immediate supervisor who can keep advancing you as they climb the professional ladder.

Bond Over Shared Interests

Pursue people with common passions at work, and you're guaranteed to catch the attention of senior executives who wouldn't pay attention to you otherwise – and no, you don't have to take up golf.

Sometimes, finding a mentor or sponsor is as easy as participating in work-related activities, including recruiting, committees, or diversity initiatives. Other times, you have to build relationships over shared interests, such as social causes or casual hobbies.

With this approach, you may first develop a sort of personal relationship. But as you interact and spend more time together, the potential mentor or sponsor may observe certain qualities that impress them.

Interactions based on mutual interests and common passions let you develop a sense of comfort and familiarity with each other. And the mentor/sponsor realizes that they enjoy working with you. They become aware of your intrinsic qualities and become convinced they can nurture your strengths and attributes to make you successful in better roles.

Trust The Process

Establishing mutual trust and respect in your professional relationships requires a certain degree of effort. Remember that forming valuable relationships takes time, even if you don't connect with colleagues immediately.

Do not put too much pressure on the people you're trying to form a working relationship with. Instead, trust the process and focus on adding quality people to your network. Get to know your colleagues as you increase your comfort levels with everyone.

Expanding Your Professional Network

One mistake I have seen far too many people make is restricting their networking attempts within their place of employment. This can be a pricey mistake, and I want to ensure you don't fall victim to that self-limiting belief. Contrary to popular belief, you can find mentors, sponsors, and advisors in any professional setting within the industry you're pursuing success in.

The strategies below can help you expand your professional network to build a personal brand, grow your career, and achieve your goals.

- ### *Attend Networking Events And Trade Shows*

This is easily one of the best ways to grow your professional network. Networking events are organized for professionals with similar interests to meet and discuss their interests. They offer a perfect growth opportunity for your career. You can easily find events in your area through LinkedIn, Eventbrite, Meetup, and other platforms designed for professionals to find events. Run a quick search of your industry or career field, and you'll encounter several network events happening in the future.

- ### *Join Professional Organizations*

Regardless of your field or industry, you would likely find different professional organizations you could join. Being a member of a professional organization is an opportunity to work with like-minded people to advance the success of your field. The best thing about this is that you're bound to connect with professionals with years of knowledge, experience, and connections that they are willing to share with the right person.

Joining a professional organization allows you to establish valuable relationships while furthering your knowledge and expertise in your field and career.

- ### *Expand Beyond Your Industry*

The worst mistake you can make as someone looking to expand their professional network is to limit yourself to your specific industry. Networking shouldn't be limited to people or events tailored to your career.

What special interest or hobby are you passionate about? You can attend events related to that as well. While establishing a professional network comprising people in your industry is crucial, there's value in expanding that network to include those who may not be in the same field but share common passions with you.

- ***Volunteer***

Pursuing volunteer opportunities with charities or advocacy groups that champion causes you're passionate about is one of the surest ways to build and expand your professional network. One con of networking events is that most are limited to small talk, which can be frustrating if you want to create deeper connections with those with similar interests.

In contrast, volunteer work allows you to have more substantial discussions, which leads to stronger and deeper relationship building. Plus, you get to meet people of diverse backgrounds. That allows you to build a stronger network that isn't just limited to your professional interests.

- ***Ask Within Your Network***

Perhaps my favorite thing about having social currency is how people are willing to facilitate valuable connections for you. Please don't be afraid or shy to ask people within your existing network to introduce you to people they know. Some are even happy to mentor you in the art of enriching your professional relationships.

Sadly, bragging about yourself to people you don't know can get a little awkward. So, Why not take it a step further and get a "networking wingman"? Essentially, this is a friend willing to talk up your achievements and successes to potential mentors and sponsors. In return, you can do the same for them.

- ***Take Advantage of LinkedIn***

LinkedIn is a social media site that has greatly made professional networking easier. Many professionals now rely on building a LinkedIn network for introductions, referrals, reviews, and references – which you can take advantage of when looking for a new job or making a major step toward career advancement.

You can use LinkedIn to stack up your professional contacts. I suggest adding anyone with a shared professional interest in your state and local area to your LinkedIn network. Any of these people can become valuable allies in the future.

Also, this site offers you a great opportunity to learn more about professionals in your industry. It is a perfect space to learn about their educational and professional backgrounds. Let's say you have a meeting with someone you hope to impress – a brief scan through their LinkedIn profile will provide conversation topics and interests to bond over.

- ### *Alumni Networks*

You can join your school's alumni association if you're a college graduate. Alumni groups are typically tasked with organizing networking events for graduates of the same school. Like networking and volunteering events, alumni networking events offer you a chance to meet professionals from varying fields with similar interests.

Most people think of alum events as an opportunity to rekindle fond (or not-so-fond) memories. Still, you can use them to discover new professional opportunities. Plus, alums tend to be generous in helping their fellow graduates. That's not an opportunity you want to waste.

- ### *Nurture Your Professional Relationships*

Professional networking isn't a one-time deal where you find a contact or advisor and then reach out to them only when you need their help. Real connections are built by nurturing sustainable, give-and-take relationships.

If you meet someone and there's a rapport, stay in touch. It would help if you put in the effort and regularly re-engage them. The conversations should flow smoothly and naturally, but you have to make a conscious effort to re-engage. Everyone is way too busy to do these things effortlessly.

While social media might seem ideal for nurturing your professional relationships, especially with people you don't work with, authentic connections are built through in-person meetings – these add depth. Developing mutual trust without personal interactions steeped in face-to-face conversations is difficult.

As you work on building your social currency and finding a mentor, sponsor, and advisor, remember to focus on personal growth. Humans are wired to help those who show a willingness to help themselves.

Always build a foundation first – learn as much as professionally acceptable about the other person and share information about yourself. In addition, don't be selfish in your networking attempts. While asking for favors is okay, I don't recommend jumping the gun straight to that. You need to establish a strong relationship first.

Building a professional social currency should be authentic and a key part of your business and professional life.

Chapter Six: Do Not Pledge Allegiance to Cliques and Groups, But Also Don't Cut Them Off

> *Honesty and integrity are a "given" in most organizations, rarely tested on any but the most superficial levels."*
>
> Paul Babiak.

Office politics turn many of us in the corporate world off. Every industry has its share of professionals who find politics in the workplace distasteful and unnecessary. I, personally, think it's murky waters.

But office politics are, unfortunately, a permanent part of the corporate world. So, it's best to learn how to navigate your workplace's political situations effectively. That is the difference between job success and failure for most people.

It's nearly impossible to win in office politics, but you can protect yourself against falling prey to cliques and groups. That way, you can minimize the potentially detrimental effects of office politics on your career.

Office politics is when a group of workers engages in activities that advance their personal agenda rather than the team's or company's agenda, usually at others' expense. It can undermine the workplace and breed catastrophe if left unchecked.

In many cases, these groups employ negative tactics to paint themselves as the good guys and make others look bad. Examples of office politics include:

- Gossiping
- Rumor mongering
- Backstabbing coworkers
- Withholding information that can affect the performance of others
- Forming cliques and alliances against colleagues
- Letting other employees fail at their job without help
- Cause other employees failures in purpose

Employees believe that fair treatment, equitable compensation, and ethical standards are a company's three most important considerations. But office politics undermine this by breeding a toxic workplace where fairness and ethical behavior are not a part of the company culture.

I talked to a few workers in different types of professions, and asked them to describe the office politics they encounter themselves. They used the following words:

- Toxic
- Unfair
- Demotivating
- Dangerous
- Frustrating
- Harmful

These adjectives underscore how harmful office politics is to a company's culture and why you should learn how to navigate the murky waters without letting them harm you, at least when it is possible.

It's possible to practice 'good' office politics to further your team's interests. The good thing is that you can promote yourself and your career without compromising personal values or the organization. At the same time, you can stay mindful of the 'bad' politics in your workplace to protect yourself from needless suffering.

Do you know how political your workplace is?

Every workplace is political to some extent, mainly because staff brings their emotions, insecurities, needs, and ambitions into their professional space, and mostly they bring them unconsciously. All workers want to be successful at their job, but we won't always agree on what "success" means or how we can achieve it. Office politics is the result of our inability to manage these differences in opinions.

Additionally, we tend to care deeply about the decision-making process in our teams, which pushes us to try to influence other people's choices. Some are straightforward about this, while some use underhanded methods.

There is a hierarchy in every workplace, so some have more power than others – still, power can be obtained through other sources. Whatever the source of a person's power in the workplace, it's normal to seek to use or increase your power. Still, many do it in a way that attacks or reduces other people's power.

Now, consider the fact that companies have limited resources. This makes teams compete to meet their needs and goals, even when this doesn't align with the "greater good." All these factors determine the extent of political plottings in a company.

To make office politics work for you, you must accept it as an uncontestable reality. Yes, it may evolve as people join and leave the organization, but it's unlikely to disappear completely.

Then, you need to create personal strategies to identify political behavior in your organization. Subsequently, you can use the information to build a strong, supportive network. You can't completely cut yourself off from office politics; neither can you immerse yourself in it. The key is to find a balance.

Before I explain how to do this, let's briefly discuss the differences between cliques and teams.

Cliques vs. Teams

If you hoped your experience with cliques ended with high school, prepare yourself for the work environment: cliques also tend to run rampant in organizations. You must be able to identify office cliques and discern between true teamwork and a clique's exclusionary chumminess.

Cliques are small groups of people with mutual interests and a common agenda. They spend time in one another's company and exclude other workers. Every clique is linked with a common agenda, usually personal advancement of their goals and career at the detriment of others.

The difference between cliques and teams is subtle but significant. Whereas team collaborations can strengthen an individual and organization and help meet objectives, joining a clique does the opposite by affecting your corporate performance and career success.

You may be tempted to pledge your allegiance to the 'dominant' social group in your office, but know that it will likely be your worst career move. Aligning yourself with them can make you guilty by association in the face of management.

Besides, cliques can make you partner with gossip and negativity, meaning you'll be perpetuating the toxic work environment you detest. That air of exclusivity that's a hallmark trait of most cliques is toxic to people within and outside the group.

Pay attention to the subtle signs of gossip, bullying, rumor-mongering, and other activities that alienate other members of the organization. It's easy to miss out on diverse perspectives when you're a slave to cliques. And that hurts not only your team and organization but your career progression.

How to Recognize and Understand Your Office's Political Behavior

Your first step is to analyze the company chart. If you aren't familiar with the cliques in your workplace, checking the organization chart can help you map out the political power-holders and influencers. One thing about office politics is that it circumvents the formal structure. So, instead of focusing on rank or job title, sit back and observe based on the organizational chart.

Ask the following questions:

★ Who are the real office influencers?

★ Who has real power but rarely exercises it?

★ Who does everyone respect?

★ Who mentors everyone?

★ Who champions everyone?

★ Who are the brains behind the organization?

Once you understand where the real power and influence lie, your next step is to figure out the informal networks, i.e., social groups. To do this, you have to examine relationships and interactions discreetly.

Pay attention to friendships and those who struggle to interact with others. Notice whether interactions and connections are based on respect, friendship, romance, or other factors. Finally, use your information to determine how influence flows between the different cliques and parties and whether interpersonal conflicts exist.

Once you've figured out how existing structures and relationships function, you can start building your social network within the organization. In other words, you must find the right people to align yourself with and do so without pledging allegiance.

Seek relationships outside your immediate team and look in all directions – be sure to cross the hierarchy. Get to know the politically powerful people in the organization and add them to your network. Ensure you do this without employing empty flattery.

Balance is crucial. It would help if you were friendly with coworkers, managers, and executives. At the same time, you shouldn't align too closely with a specific group or another; otherwise, everyone will start assuming you're a member of that group, which can limit your access.

Office politics is about people, so you must have strong interpersonal skills. Reflect on your feelings, what triggers them, and how you deal with them. That will help you when it comes to building a strong social network.

Emotional self-regulation will help you master the art of thinking before acting. Being emotionally intelligent will also allow you to recognize other people's emotions and approach them in easier ways.

For many, their first instinct is to avoid coworkers who practice "bad" politics in the workplace. These people don't know that it only makes them a target. It's much better to "keep your friends close and enemies even closer" when it comes to office politics.

So, get familiar with your workplace gossip, bullies, and manipulators. Be courteous with them but guarded at the same time. Don't say things that they might put a negative spin on. You can familiarize yourself with the goals of these people's politicking so that you can protect yourself or counter the effects. And remember that many people engage in negativity due to insecurity.

Protecting yourself by avoiding negativity is the best thing you can do for yourself. But what if you take it a step further by neutralizing negative politics? That way, you can contribute to making your workplace significantly more positive.

Choose the 'secrets' you share carefully. For example, don't pass on rumors without carefully considering the source, credibility, and impact. Also, don't expect people to keep the things you share confidential. You're safer if you assume that whatever you share will be repeated.

Be professional at all times. Avoid taking sides or getting sucked into recriminations and arguments. When you find yourself in a conflict, remember there's no winning or losing. The best option is to find a solution that satisfies all parties involved in the conflict.

Now that you know how to identify the cliques and groups in your company, how do you deal with them?

How to Deal With Cliques

You may be unable to change the corporate culture because you're just one person. Still, you can do your part to uplift others and manage groups effectively. Dealing with cliques ensures that the informal structures in your workplace exist for the greater good, not just for the interest of a few people.

➢ Do lunch

Food is a powerful organizing process that can effectively unite people, even in the workplace. Go out to lunch with your coworkers, both newbies and veterans. Eating lunch together is one of the best ways to open up a close group and get to know your coworkers deeper. Look for people you don't usually associate with at work and invite a few of them to lunch or coffee – they'll like you for it. If there is any gossip or negative comments about anything, you don't need to agree or disagree. You can just accept the information, don't judge, and remain friendly enough to make it clear that you respectfully don't want to get involved.

➢ Get closer

This strategy is for managers. By reducing the physical distance between workstations, you can bust the cliques in your workplace. You might have noticed that many of these tightly knit cliques typically form around employee workstations that are far apart. If you can move some of these around, you might be able to break them open. And even if you aren't a manager, moving your desk near these groups can help you strike up conversations. That will help with networking.

➢ Take a break

Many managers don't know this, but the 'break structure' in a company contributes to how much the cliques thrive. As a manager, you can align the breaks of colleagues on the same team to help them break into cliques. Doing this will increase cohesion and performance gains due to improved information sharing within the groups.

Suppose there's a particularly nasty clique in your office, and you've done your best to network with them to no success. In that case, it might be time to look for the next opportunity. It also helps to know when to give up and move on from a toxic corporate culture.

Whether we like it or not, office politics are a fact of the corporate world. If you avoid it altogether, you will most likely find yourself without a voice in your workplace. Even worse, you give people with less knowledge, experience, and skills than you the chance to influence decisions that can affect you, your team, and your career.

Having Empathy vs. Suffering from Others' Pain

Empathy is the ability to feel other people's emotions as if they were yours. Empathy does not mean assuming people's feelings, agreeing with them, or going out of your way to protect them. It's putting yourself in someone else's shoes. But that doesn't mean you have to suffer other people's pain. You can be empathetic without taking on someone's pain.

The ability to "feel with" people's emotions is a beautiful gift that allows us to connect with other people. Yet it can become unbearable and distressing at times. Your empathic response can shift toward empathic distress, which involves suffering from someone else's pain.

Empathic distress traps you in suffering because it is a self-focused response to another person's pain. If you frequently experience empathic distress, working in a toxic environment with gossip and negative politics is probably the hardest thing you'll ever have to do. But the good thing is you can protect yourself and shift to empathic concern instead with the strategies below.

- Check in with yourself regularly. When you feel distressed in response to someone else's pain, take a few deep breaths and tune in with your feelings. Figure out what you need and the right way to respond to that person.
- Appraise your thoughts and feelings if you feel particularly distressed by the person's struggle. Reflect on your interpretation of the event or situation. This will help to reduce feelings of anxiety, both physically and emotionally.
- Name your feelings to trusted friends or coworkers. Expressing your feelings to others can reduce empathic distress, especially when prioritizing non-violent communication.

- Respond to people with compassion. Unlike empathic distress, compassion and empathic concern are cut from the same cloth. Both involve concern for someone's suffering and a desire to relieve their pain.

Knowing how to navigate difficult emotions and respond to people with compassion can make you more resilient at work and in other aspects of your life.

Strategies For Dealing With Office Gossip

You should be aware of the different ways to deal with gossip in the workplace. Choosing not to waste your time with office gossip is wise, but don't be surprised if bullies and gossips attack you for this decision.

Gossip is a poisonous plant: feed it, and it will grow. Eventually, it will reach more people, and you may be unable to stop it. On the other hand, starve it, and you'll nip it in the bud. If a coworker approaches you with gossip, respectfully respond to them with a positive perspective. That will make the coworker think twice about defaming their colleagues.

So, let's say that a colleague comes to you with gossip about your immediate supervisor. This person says awful things about the supervisor, highlights their flaws, demeans them, and harshly criticizes their decisions and behavior. You may have two different views about this:

1st: You don't share the same perspective. In fact, you admire your supervisor as he/she is.

2nd: You agree with the colleague's view and hold grudges about the supervisor's behavior and actions.

Despite what you might feel, the best approach to this is to respond with positive things about the supervisor. If you also have a negative view of the supervisor, doing this might be hard.

However, I want you to practice this exercise: focus on the positives no matter how hard it is. Despite how bad a person might seem, you can always find redeeming qualities in them. If you focus on a healthy perspective, you will achieve a much calmer and more peaceful state of mind.

You may wonder why this exercise is important. The reason is that when you speak of negativity, you taint your subconscious mind with toxicity. You will internalize what you said, making you feel bad even if you don't reflect on your words.

But when you focus on the good and redeeming qualities, you take a compassionate and empathetic approach to dealing with the gossiper. That can inspire the gossiper to view the supervisor's actions from a better perspective.

For example, you may respond by saying, "Actually, it's OK if they make a few mistakes. We're all humans and don't know what the other person is going through outside of work. I think we should all try to be more compassionate. I also do things that might displease some people, so I don't want to judge another person. I hope you understand my perspective."

Sure, this response might put you in the gossiper's line of attack for a while because they couldn't get you to participate in their toxicity. But it might also make them rethink their pattern of approaching colleagues to gossip about others and possibly change that habit.

The secret to coping with gossiping coworkers is to approach them with respect. It would be best if you made it clear that you aren't interested in taking sides and that you're comfortable enough to share your point of view with them.

At first, they might feel rejected since they are probably not used to getting a response like that. So, there might be some clashes. But, eventually, they will start seeing it from a different perspective and feel confident enough to share their opinions with you, but with a new approach.

If you use this positive strategy to deal with gossip, you can make that happen. I'm confident you'll feel rewarded for doing your part in improving the culture at your organization.

Your other option is to cut the gossiping coworker off. However, if you resolve every issue by cutting people off, you might garner a reputation as a hateful person. People might come to avoid you due to the lack of tolerance and diplomacy.

If you can handle a neutral relationship with office gossip without getting drained or exhausted, I say you go for it. Cutting toxic people off becomes an option if you find the negativity mentally and emotionally harmful. But it's ultimately your choice to make. You're the only person who understands your limit.

Sometimes, it becomes nearly impossible to handle toxic situations at work. When this happens, you start to experience a burnout sensation that's potentially dangerous for your mental and physical health, and might result in losing your job.

What should you do when you find yourself edging too close to disastrous levels of stress and exhaustion? How do you handle burnout?

Find a comprehensive answer to these questions in the next chapter.

Chapter Seven: Burnout Indicators

> *"Plans are useless; planning is everything. Planning means knowing where you are, where you want to go, and every contingency between point A, to point B. Workers should be protected and helped, not overwhelmed by unplanned strategies."*

John Shook.

John Shook, the first American hired by Toyota, a Japanese company whose challenge in the 1980s was the globalization of its business, dominated North American geography. With that, his challenge was to implement NUMMI in the United States. What was surprising is that the executives already knew the huge challenge they had and used their wise tools and planning to avoid stress beforehand. And we're talking about the 80s; the Japanese already had this emotional understanding.

The Japanese culture acted in a humble way, assuming to the industry that they had no foresight of what could happen, unlike the Americans' approach to competitors, trying to show a greater market power than it really is.

Toyota's plan with the manufacturer NUMMI, the future responsible for producing the model Corolla and Tacoma, was to understand the American market and expand its brand. And the company didn't want the line workers to play a role in improving the designs themselves. They should stop the assembly line immediately if they see a problem to escalate to a more accurate assessment of the problem. In other words, the objective was not time and haste, putting pressure on workers to fix small problems on their own, but focusing on quality and precision in the satisfactory result of production. This means that management prevents overwork and employee burnout in favor of the mental and physical health of all company members.

Burnouts can take a huge toll on your daily activities. When you're burned out, you lack energy, are mentally exhausted, unmotivated, and uninterested.

Most adults spend most of the day at work. So, if you despise working with your boss and colleagues, hate going to work, and don't feel fulfilled with what you're doing, it can hurt you. You'll get burned out! Even if you enjoy your work, being under a lot of stress for an extended time can cause burnout.

Your burnout could even interfere with your ability to think and process information accordingly if it's not handled.

There was a time in my life when I was exhausted. Everything seemed to irritate me. The sound of car horns, the chirping of birds, the sight of people, and even silence got me upset.

Every morning, I woke up with no zeal to continue the day. I just wanted to lock myself in the room and sleep all day. I flared up at the slightest provocation and was moody the whole day.

I didn't know how bad it was till my best friend offered to take me out for lunch, and I refused. I would never refuse my best friend; why was I doing it now? My best friend insisted and came to my house to drag me out.

We had a long conversation that day. He told me of all the changes he had noticed in me, and I couldn't deny them. They were true! I hadn't gotten a haircut in a long time, and my facial expression showed a lack of will for the simplest things. I was always so grumpy, sad, and quiet.

I poured out my heart to him. I told him how I was bothered about my job and finances, how much time I spent in that place feeling like nothing, feeling like a small particle of that company, making money for someone else that didn't care about who I was or what were my deepest abilities, and how I barely had enough time to rest my mind.

I knew I was not happy where I was, but my bills didn't let me stop going to work. Even though I knew that was definitely not my purpose in life. I was burned out! My friend encouraged me and gave me a list of things to try out. I'll talk about them later in this chapter. For now, let's talk about you.

Sometimes you just want to take a breather– throw in the towel and sleep for two weeks straight. Well, then do it! Sometimes your body is simply responding to your dissatisfaction, stress, and overload.

What Are Burn-Out Indicators?

Think about those times you lose your appetite for your favorite foods. Or you yell and walk out on your colleagues at the slightest provocation. What sets this attitude off? Do the following statements ring a bell?

- ▯ I have too many things on my plate; I can't do it all.
- ▯ My team is counting on me, and I can't take it anymore.
- ▯ I'm not comfortable saying to anyone that it is too much for me.

- My boss will fire me if I fail. I can't leave this task behind or delegate it.

If so, you struggle with stress. You either suffer from overload or the wrong kinds of stress. Either way, you're burned out. Anger and impatience are your way of expressing burnout. Some people would withdraw when stressed, and others would say unkind things.

Burnout indicators can take two forms. They're the active and the passive form. By passive indicators, I mean emotional and mental exhaustion. For example, being unable to think well or concentrate, getting triggered or frustrated easily. These are all passive indicators of burnout.

On the other hand, active indicators of burnout mean physical exhaustion. You'll get tired easily; feel sleepy, dizzy, weak, and lazy all day.

This friend of mine, who is an Architect, told me a recent story at that time: "*I was appointed the team leader for a project in my workplace. The project is one of the most significant projects the company I worked with at the time had ever undertaken. Hence, it had to be led by someone with considerable experience and expertise.*

Other people could lead the team better than I could. However, the director chose me because he believed in my ability to pull off the project. When I walked out of his office, I echoed his mantra in my mind, 'You can do this.'.

I began to lead the team with enthusiasm and determination. The devotion of my team members spurred me to get better. They came up with practical ideas and followed them up.

There was never a point where I felt that I was handling the project alone. My team members took their assigned responsibilities seriously. Some even went out of their way to ensure our plans panned out.

I was shocked when we wanted to present the outcome before the board of directors. I had 9 team members; only one person showed up. That one person countered every single statement I made during the presentation. She claimed that there was no team spirit and that I made every decision independently. Hence, the other eight members refused to show up.

The board was watching. I couldn't afford to succumb to pressure. So I didn't let those false remarks get the best of me. However, towards the end of the presentation, I received a phone call from one of my team members that our sponsors had withdrawn their financial support for the project. So my prolonged efforts for over three months had gone down the drain.

I had mixed emotions of sadness, anger, and inadequacy. Suddenly, my vision became blurry, and my legs numbed. Before I knew it, I collapsed in the boardroom. This is a combo of active and passive indicators of burnout."

Listening to my friend telling me about that awful experience, I went after some information about how this burnout effects start, and how it develops, so I could try to avoid them.

Passive Indicators of Burnout

You're working hard and trying to build a career you admire. But at some point, you became tired of trying. Then you started feeling cynical about the future. Could it be a passive indicator of burnout?

Passive burnout is a collection of different psychological and emotional reactions that occur in response to stress overload.

You must know the symptoms/indicators of passive burnout. It can impact enthusiasm, productivity, social skills, problem-solving, and creativity. Passive burnouts can also be associated with several mental health problems, such as depression, insomnia, anxiety, and short attention span.

The early indicators of passive burnout include pessimism, a negative attitude to work, feeling like you're wasting your time on a specific project, and many others.

We all face mental challenges at work. However, they can become impregnable for people experiencing passive burnout. People experiencing this type of burnout may withdraw from work. They feel like their best is not good enough. Or maybe they feel that they will always have the same ridiculous results even if they continue to try. This kind of attitude can manifest as chronic depression.

It would be best if you also looked for the slightest clues about their sadness and hopelessness in their languages. For example, words such as "why try?", "Me against the world," "working with them is like a death sentence," and deep sighs accompany many others.

Have you been missing deadlines, coming late to work, violating rules, or withdrawing from tasks you used to like? These could be other indicators of passive burnout in people who don't ordinarily do that.

If allowed to aggravate, it can have negative effects on your coworkers. This includes shutting coworkers up when they have ideas, cursing them unnecessarily, and many others.

You're also burned out passively when you take subtle steps to avoid solving more problems.

Active Indicators of Burnout

Active indicators of burnout are collections of different physical reactions in response to prolonged stress.

Unlike the passive indicators of burnout, it's easy to spot their active counterparts. This is because they include physical symptoms. However simple it may seem, it's also important to be able to spot the symptoms of active burnout. This is because it can seriously affect your physical and mental health.

Physical health issues associated with active burnout include stroke, cardiac death, prolonged fatigue, headaches, heart disease, respiratory issues, eating disorders, alcohol poisoning, and many others. The early indicators of active burnout include adopting negative coping techniques such as unhealthy drinking or eating habits.

Employees that experience active burnout may try to get drunk every day after work to drown their sorrows. They may also temporarily engage in binge eating episodes to get through their thoughts.

In most cases, burnout's passive and active indicators express themselves together. So let's call this point of convergence "the general indicators." The warning signs of the general indicators of burnout include being easily pissed off and expressing impatience. For some people, this is their usual behavior. However, it may indicate chronic stress in people who are usually calm and collected.

If these signs are ignored, it can lead to more subtle behaviors such as frequent crying at the slightest exchange of words with coworkers.

People experiencing active burnout can hurt their colleagues even more than passive ones. It ruins team spirit and work relationships.

The 5 Rules To Treat and Prevent Burnout

It's better to prevent burnout than to try to get over it. The following techniques are surefire ways to help you to identify burnouts quickly and prevent the worst episodes. It'll also help you to stay in control if it has already taken a huge toll on you.

Remember, the first rule is that you should spot the passive and active indicators of burnout. Get a journal and write out how you feel. Next, write out the active or passive indicators you've been experiencing.

You must know that passive burnout scales up quickly to active counterparts. Hence, they make one another worse.

For example, feelings of hopelessness can lead to drinking. It can also lead to frequent angry outbursts. You should identify these indicators. Know yourself well enough to figure out when things are about to get out of hand.

The second rule is that you need to keep an open mind. It'll be nearly impossible to manage burnout if you're unwilling to break free from it.

The third rule of thumb is to think twice before acting. Ask yourself; what happened in the past and right now and why? Stop and think about the triggers if burnout has occurred. Maybe you're trying to meet unrealistic deadlines. Then ask yourself again: how do I pause this pressure?

The fourth rule is to use good social contact. You can reach out to your partner, like-minded persons or associations, friends, and family members you trust. Spend quality time with them.

Do you feel weird about this last tip? You don't have to. After speaking with my best friend, I felt much better. He even promised to check up and give me the emotional support I needed at the time.

The trick is that opening up doesn't make you a liability to other people. On the contrary, your loved ones will be happy that you're reaching out, strengthening your bond.

The people you reach out to may not fix the source of your impending burnout. They just need to be excellent listeners. Then, you'll easily get over your burnout and regain the feelings of appreciating yourself again.

Also, ensure that you stay away from negative-minded people, especially colleagues at work. They're bad for your healing process. They do nothing but lower your morale. If you need to work with them, you shouldn't spend too much time around them.

If preventing burnout seems like a pipe dream, you should take a break from work. You could go on a weekend vacation with your partner or request a temporary leave of absence. Just do anything to unwind. Do something different. Go to a place you've never been to before. Utilize the break to regain your energy and try new adventures.

It wouldn't be bad to meditate and get enough sleep. It'll activate your body's relaxation response. You can also try yoga and deep breathing exercises to bounce back.

The Difference Between Self-Flagellation And Self-Compassion

My journey into self-compassion has been a process of becoming and letting go. It feels like a sort of gradual detoxification from poisonous feelings.

Think about when you hit your head against the wall, smacked, and blamed yourself for losing a contract with a potential client. This is self-flagellation. Self-flagellation means you're criticizing or torturing yourself openly for your problems.

On the other hand, self-compassion means embracing your problems and striving to move on. You believe that torturing yourself is unnecessary for ultimate well-being and progress.

A self-compassionate person will treat himself to a nice dinner after losing his job. It doesn't mean that he's happy about his circumstances. He just believes that there are better opportunities out there for him.

Self-Compassion requires a high level of self-trust and inner strength. Thankfully, these can be developed through constant practice.

Unlike self-compassion, self-flagellation reduces growth. Of course, it helps you to own up to your mistakes or problems. But it'll lead to a lack of self-confidence, insecurity, self-destructive actions, and many others.

A self-flagellated person is prone to depression, leading to suicidal thoughts.

We might skip relaxation time and fun activities in our drive to accomplish great things. We tend to ignore the symptoms of burnout until we become ill. This is also self-flagellation. You're torturing yourself.

Many of us don't realize the many ways we torture ourselves every day. We constantly pull an all-nighter all in the name of work. We eat less and exercise less.

These days, self-compassion might not be the trend. But, it brings positive vibes to your workplace and society. Extending compassion to others wouldn't be difficult when everyone has compassion for themselves.

Say no to practices that only serve to demotivate you. Also, tell yourself that you can do better instead of succumbing to mediocrity. When you treat yourself with compassion, you develop a growth mindset. You know that you're constantly evolving and wouldn't beat yourself too hard if your plans fail.

How Can Self-Compassion Help You?

Experiencing setbacks in your workplace can be very frustrating. It can make you lose your mind if not addressed carefully. Knowing this, your response to this situation is very important.

Often, what determines the outcome of a situation is your reaction. Your response to a situation can tilt the odds in the long run.

Most adults react to these situations by lashing out at their loved ones or shutting off their inner circle. Relax! This issue is not the end of the world.

Now that you've encountered this situation, how will you approach it? It's simple. Just be compassionate to yourself. Breathe. Take your time.

How can you do this? Imagine how you'd treat your close friend in a similar situation. Imagine how you'd encourage him not to be judgemental but be kind to himself. Now apply these theories to yourself.

Self-compassion allows you to be kind to yourself even when you experience burnout. It allows you to recognize setbacks as a temporary phase in your pursuit of success.

- **Self-compassion will help you find inner peace.**

Finding inner peace is very vital to your mental health. You can only do well at work when you have a sound mind. When your mind is troubled, anxiety sets in; If this anxiety overwhelms you, depression can set in too. You might also start feeling like a shadow of yourself.

If you find yourself in this situation, you need to be compassionate. Self-compassion will help you understand that you need to put yourself first. Also, you'll learn to let go of some situations. Consequently, you'll find the inner peace you need.

- **Self-compassion will help you develop a growth mindset.**

A growth mindset means acknowledging that you can develop your skills and intelligence. Self-compassion is very important for this to happen. Self-compassion is the first phase when you're working on your personal growth. The self-compassion phase is your reflection phase. It's the period where you come to terms with your true self, acknowledging who you are and what you can offer and giving room for improvement.

Treating yourself with compassion makes you likely to give yourself time to improve and not limit yourself to your current situation.

➢ Self-compassion builds your self-confidence.

Building your self-confidence is difficult, especially when you're burned out or experiencing a setback in your workplace. So when you start muttering statements like "I don't think I can do this anymore," "I can't do anything right at work, "you need to start caring for yourself deeply. Nevertheless, as you treat yourself with care and compassion, you begin to create a sense of self-worth. Gradually, you're building your self-confidence.

You'll realize that you're more proud of your skills, and you can now confidently take on more tasks in your workplace with an aura of positivity around you.

Stay True To Yourself

Most people tend to drift off their true selves to suit the dynamics in their workplace. They seem to think it's the only way they can match up to their workplace regularities. Well, they couldn't be farther from the truth.

The truth is that your best comes with your true self. Your true self expresses itself in your interactions with coworkers, productivity, and response to setbacks.

Your relationship with your coworkers is perhaps the most important part of your workplace. When the relationship between you and your coworker turns sour, it becomes a tense zone for you.

Now that you know how important your relationship with your coworkers is, how else do you think you can connect with them deeply? By staying true to yourself; this way, you form an original bond with them. They'll be able to accept you for who you are.

Your productivity in your workplace also needs your true self. So even when you miss your target numbers, you'll be able to respond to the situation positively.

You don't have to suppress your personality and get stuck in your job. When your temperament and personality suit your job, you'll enjoy what you do. You can only achieve these by staying true to yourself.

Chapter Eight: Failure Is A Temporary Friend

“Your economic security does not lie in your job; it lies in your own power to produce - to think, to learn, to create, to adapt.”

Stephen R. Covey.

It’s worth mentioning a short bit of Stephen R. Covey from his bestseller ***7 habits of Highly Effective People***:

“Your physical health affects your mental health; your spiritual strength affects your social/emotional strength. As you improve in one dimension, you increase your ability in other dimensions as well. As you renew your physical dimension, you reinforce your personal vision, the paradigm of your own self-awareness and free will, of proactivity, of knowing that you are free to act, failing instead of being acted upon, to choose your own response to any stimulus. As you renew your mental dimension, you reinforce your personal management.”

Renovation And Balance

Nobody wants to fail; we can start from there!

We all want to be known for good things – have a portfolio of outstanding successes and no failures. I used to want that too. But now, I've come to terms with the fact that failure is inevitable, sometimes necessary. Running away from failure is like running away from life itself.

We've all experienced failure at a point in our lives. Maybe not at work or school, but maybe the time you cooked a terrible meal or when you promised someone a gift and didn't get it for them. What I've learned is that failure doesn't matter. What matters is how you react to it. This mindset has changed me for good.

Failure and success in the same sentence sound very controversial and absurd. Yet, they're like two brothers, both at opposite ends of a line, connected yet far apart.

Failure Isn't A Curse

Think of a time when you failed. Maybe you failed a course or performed terribly during a presentation. How did it make you feel? What did you do? It doesn't matter how bad your presentation was. Instead, be concerned about the lessons you learned from the presentation and how you'll use them moving forward.

When I was younger, I would sulk and cry till I fell ill. It was the only way I reacted to failure. But, growing up, I now know that if I'm not doing anything to make the story better, then all my crying is pointless.

Take a quick look at the lives of successful people around you. Every one of them has got a story of failure to tell. Some had many experiences failing their tasks before they finally got them right. What kept them going were the lessons they learned from the failure and how they implemented it.

These days social media scrubbing the people's best moments of their lives (which can be made up in an amazing picture) on people's faces creates an illusion sensation that we will never achieve such "happiness" if we keep failing as we do. Even worse, we fail in the simplest things; how could we manage to avoid failing with the big industries or big achievements?

Even Bill Gates, one of the world's leading men, has a record of failure. He dropped out of Harvard and co-owned a business that ended up being a total failure. But he didn't allow his setbacks to define him.

Instead, he redirected the energy into Microsoft; now it is one of the world's leading companies. He became the world's youngest self-made billionaire.

Why not think of failure as a reassurance that I can do better?

Failure can make you do two things. First, you can either decide to pick up from where you have failed and do better or decide to give up. Whichever direction you choose shapes the results you get subsequently.

Tom and Frank started new businesses separately at the same time. Coincidentally, both businesses were a disaster. They made huge losses and had to sell personal belongings to pay debts.

Tom decided to give up because he couldn't risk such a loss again. He was afraid of facing a similar outcome again. Frank, on the other hand, decided to assess the situation. He took his time to retrace his steps to find out how it all went wrong and how he could bring a positive turnaround.

He kept doing research and putting in the effort to change the situation. Finally, Frank made significant profits from the same business after a year.

Do you brood every day because things didn't go as planned, or do you sit up and take reasonable action to change the circumstances? When you fail, you should think of how to improve, not sit there whining and whimpering all day long.

Every time we fail, we reduce ourselves to the extent of that failure. We don't acknowledge that we're much more than the failure that hit us. I tell you that just like the teenage years, failure is a phase! It'll be over soon enough. When it hits, acknowledge that it's for the time being and that you'll bounce back.

I once had to write a professional exam. It was very important for my promotion in my workplace. Unfortunately, I failed one of the papers I sat for woefully. It was a very difficult phase for me. I didn't see it coming at all. I was down and out.

I already had my life for the next year planned out, and it didn't include rewriting an exam I failed. I was angry for a while but got over it quickly because I wanted to get promoted at work.

I picked up my books, dusted them, and returned to them. I recognized the setback as a phase. With renewed hope, I believed I'd rewrite the exam and ace it. And guess what? I wrote the exam again and passed it this time with flying colors.

If you see failure as the end of the road for you, it'll be. It's all about the perspective you have. If you overcome the failure and leave it behind to give it another go, that failure will transform into an experience. But if you keep reminding yourself and highlighting that failure, with self-flagellation, it becomes a dark cloud over your head, disturbing your willingness to try again, and believe you can do better.

The 10 Secrets Of Coping With Failure

Failure is what you make out of it. So you shouldn't expect anything to change if you decide to hang in there, complaining to others about how you could have done better.

Instead of dwelling on pain of failure, you should find ways to make the most of it. You can rise high if you adopt these coping mechanisms.

- ***Allow yourself to feel every emotion.***

One of my childhood friends got fired from where she had worked for five years. She had put in so much work but made a huge mistake that ended her contract. She felt grief, disappointment, disbelief, and hurt because she couldn't wrap her mind around losing her job.

Every Friday night, she took to clubbing and drank to a stupor. She refused to talk to anyone about what she was going through. It wasn't very pleasant, so she kept quiet. Gradually, Anna slipped into a deep depression phase. She refused to eat and isolated herself from everyone. She later recovered but with intense treatment of therapy and medication.

She wouldn't have reached that state if she'd faced her emotions and met them head-on. Maybe if she had allowed herself to feel all the emotions, she would've handled everything better.

This is a cue to free yourself. Cry if you have to. Scream if you need to. As long as no one is getting hurt, express yourself. Don't run away from how you feel. If you want to heal, then you have to feel first, and then understand what happened to you, and what caused that emotion. Embrace your emotions. Feel it, whether it's anger, shame, pain, anxiety, or fear. If you run away from your emotions, they'll come back to haunt you. It might be a lot for you to handle at first, but it'll pay off in the end.

Brennan Manning, in one of his quotes, once said: *"To affirm a person is to see the good in them that they cannot see in themselves and to repeat it in spite of appearances to the contrary. Please, this is not some Pollyanna optimism that is blind to the reality of evil, but rather like a fine radar system that is tuned in to the true, the good, and the beautiful."* I once read an amazing book written by Brennan, called *The Impostor Who Lives In Me*. In that context, I've learned about the Impostor Syndrome; this is an approach that made me understand that as soon as we accept the way our emotions react, and our inner "monsters" exist, they will slowly fade away. But if you neglect them and pretend it doesn't exist, that will, for sure, strongly disturb you.

The impostor syndrome also makes us feel like a fraud because we tend to hide these "monsters" from the ones around us. When we learn to accept them and expose them without the fear of being judged, these monsters go away and leave us alone to be our true selves, in peace of mind. You then don't feel guilty with the mask of fraud, and you get to be transparent with everyone.

○ ***Don't cover pain with unhealthy practices.***

When you feel pain, you might be tempted to cover it up. Pretend it didn't affect you and make others believe you've moved on with life. Sometimes you want to be like my friend and just party all week, eat junk, drink alcohol wildly, consume drugs frequently, or oversleep. You want to make yourself numb with the hope that it covers up how you feel.

These are terrible ways to deal with pain. Yes, the pain of failure can be overwhelming, but emotions are emotions because they're to be felt. These unhealthy practices can become habits, and they will only give you a reprieve.

After you party all night and get home drunk, you'll wake up with a headache. Your situation is still the same, or maybe worse. Drinking too much alcohol and eating junk will make you gain weight. You'll also begin to hate your body, pushing you deeper into depression. Diverting your attention to unhealthy coping mechanisms won't help your situation. They'd only make you feel better for a minute and worse for an hour. It is like a downfalling snowball in the mountain; it increases and escalates wildly.

- ***Handle your pain the healthy way.***

People react to failure differently. For example, you could take a walk on a sunny afternoon to clear your head, take a bubble bath, attend family events, and speak to a professional.

Whichever way you choose, you must consider two factors. First, ensure that you aren't suppressing your emotions. The other is that you do it the right and healthy way. Get a new hobby, talk to a friend about how you feel, visit an old friend or do something you love.

If it's difficult to follow healthy practices, drawing a list could help. On the list, you could put together various activities for yourself that could fast-track your healing process. It'll also help if you put this list in an easily noticeable place. This would remind you daily of the necessary actions you need to take to get the desired results.

- ***Put irrational beliefs and pride aside.***

Your thoughts are what hold you back. Your whole life is centered on how you think and what you think. If you think of failure as a chance to get better at what you do, you wouldn't be so hard on yourself when things don't go as planned.

Your whole life, you've been told how it's a terrible thing to have a failure on your record. These beliefs are very wrong and can prevent us from taking the necessary risks we should take as humans.

Set aside self-limiting thoughts and think about how much you can achieve from experience.

○ *Develop a realistic and positive outlook on failure.*

Develop a mental resilience against negative thoughts about failure. Each time you feel your thoughts moving towards the negative, reframe them. Affirm good and positive things about yourself. Remind yourself of how far you've come and how good you're doing for yourself.

Look into a mirror and say to yourself, "My failure is a sign that I'm doing something good and taking steps. Failure means I'm not stagnant. Failure has no hold on me. I can handle failure and learn from it". These can look like little statements, but the effect they could have on you would go a long way.

I remember after woefully failing that professional exam, I kept reminding myself how it wasn't that much of a big deal. My response to the failure was all that mattered. I picked up my pen and outlined all the possible mistakes I could've made. Then I realized I'd been very lazy and selective with my reading. I realized I could've prepared better, which helped me prepare for my re-sit.

Having this mindset will make it easier for you to progress. Also, while moving forward, don't set goals that aren't feasible. It'll only flop and crush your confidence back to square one.

- ***Take responsibility.***

When failures occur, our first human reaction is to make excuses. We try to find ways to excuse ourselves from what led to the failure. We blame others. My teammates left me. The computer had a problem. It's never you!

We refuse to accept that we did something wrong or that there's something we could have done better. This hinders us from learning from our mistakes. Take responsibility for the failure but don't go overboard. Don't beat yourself up constantly instead of looking for ways to turn things around. Stop living in the past.

When you look at failure, look for explanations, not excuses. Find out why it happened the way it did. This will make finding a solution to the problem easier and faster.

- ***Research famous failures.***

There're so many stories of failures from popular people and their responses to them on the internet. From Thomas Edison to Bill Gates to Walt Disney, there are so many stories you can read to help change your mindset.

Do continuous research about famous success turnaround stories, and you might be amazed that you'll find many of them recording failure more than once. Study closely the steps they took to get the change they wanted for themselves. Your story might be the next one on the internet in the future!

- ***Learn from your mistakes.***

If you're willing to learn, there's much to learn from failures. Failure can be a good teacher. Think about and write out the mistakes you think you made. Then highlight the ones that you think were the most defining mistakes.

Ask yourself what you can learn from these mistakes and what you can do differently. This way, you're sure that you have picked something significant that will help you move forward.

Instead of seeing failure as the end of life or a big burden, see it as the next step to achieving your goals.

- ***Create a plan moving forward.***

My high school teacher said, "Failing to plan is planning to fail ." So after identifying where things went wrong, you should make proper plans to move forward. Don't be afraid to try again or start all over. When the fear of trying again hits you, reaffirm that your past mistakes don't hold you down and can try again.

With the new things you've learned about your past mistakes, focus on what you can do differently to achieve better results. Then, create a solid plan that incorporates every new thing you learn.

○ ***Face the fear of failure and take the risk of trying again.***

The fear of failure always stays at the back of your mind. It haunts you and forces you to remember things you're trying to forget. Allow yourself to face that fear. Then, grab it by the neck, beat it up, and kick it out of your life.

Practice stepping out of your comfort zone. Do new things that'll test your stamina and resilience. At first, it may seem very difficult. Still, over time, you'll realize that you are no more afraid of taking risks and that the extra push you gave yourself is helping you achieve more and more of your goals.

Trying again is not as easy as it sounds, especially after a big failure, but you need to. You have to push yourself to take that risk.

Bouncing Back From Failure At Work

Failure at work can crush your confidence. You begin to imagine how your colleagues now see you as useless. You might even think of quitting your job for fear of being laid off. All these feelings are natural.

However, a well-drafted plan may not work because there's a little flaw in your plan. Your plan might be flawless but external factors you didn't think of might make it fail. This is why you should go easy on yourself.

Accept failure as a learning experience and use it to get better. It can be very challenging to experience failure at work. However, you can bounce back from a failure at work by accepting that failure is a possible outcome. You're not the first to fail at work and will not be the last. Failure isn't uncommon. Every day at different workplaces, people make big and small mistakes.

With overwhelming deadlines and loads of work piling up at desks every day, it's almost impossible not to make mistakes.

There's already work pressure; you don't need to put more pressure on yourself by dwelling so much on the mistakes you made. Instead, learn to make mistakes as a part of your work process; they're inevitable and will occur from time to time.

See failure at work as part of the learning process to improve your tasks and jobs. Remember, positive energy only! When you make mistakes at work, your ego takes a huge blow. A friend once told me he made a huge mistake that cost his company lots of money.

His team leader had brought him before the rest of the team and said so many horrible things to his face in the presence of others. He said it was such a humbling moment for him. He was ashamed and couldn't look anybody in the eye for days.

I felt so bad for him because I knew what an embarrassing situation that must have been for him. So, I asked him what he did to make a change. He said he worked tirelessly and relentlessly on the next project. He stayed some nights at the office to perfect his tasks and avoid future mistakes.

It eventually paid off because the project was a huge success. He even got recognized not just by his team leader for his outstanding contribution but also by the company's CEO.

Don't let one mistake make you a negative person. What if he had given up and resigned from work just because the embarrassment was just too much?

Reflect on mistakes and think of possible solutions to change the situation. In a bid to encourage me, my best friend told me of his experience at his workplace, how everyone on his team turned on him and blamed him for a project that was supposed to be teamwork. He became the scapegoat even though he wasn't the only one that made mistakes.

For weeks, people kept talking, and some even grumbled when they assigned new tasks to him. He didn't let these get to him, though. You shouldn't either. People would always talk. People are always projecting their fears onto others. Negativity would come from all sides. However, it would be best if you didn't let small talk bother you. Do your thing. You're not the only person to make a mistake.

Allow yourself time to reflect, learn from your errors, and move forward. Accept your mistakes and take responsibility for fixing them. Don't push the blame on others for mistakes you made. Don't make excuses for yourself too. Instead, accept that you're at fault and do what is necessary to change that!

The approach to coping with failure is to reflect, admit, apply and repeat. Reflect on the mistakes you made. Admit that you made mistakes and take responsibility for your mistake. Own up to your mistakes. Apply what you have learned from your mistakes and think of ways forward.

Chapter Nine: The Key To Train Yourself To Stay Positive

It is not enough that we just recognize that we are imperfect; it is necessary for us to be self-aware, to go inside, and find our own being in deeper layers. Mapping our mental ghosts is essential to combating false beliefs and creating a state of mind potent in positivity and optimism."

The very first step is to renounce the attempt to be perfect, without emotional crises or destabilizations.

Everyone has bad days, days where everything seems to be out of control, and you may want to cry or sleep all day. It's hard to remain calm and positive in the face of trouble. At times like these, our problems blind us, and we can't find the positive side of every pain. But, the positive sides are always there. You just need to sit up and learn how to find them.

Negativity shouldn't rule your world. It's a choice, not your lifeline. Why choose to be sad when you can be happy? Some people live under the worst conditions but are still genuinely happy by choice. How? By choosing to focus on the bright side, training to respond to the triggers of the mind.

Your colleagues may tell you that you're not up to the task. Your boss might discredit your work and demean you. But those negative remarks shouldn't dictate how you feel about yourself. Don't let these words dampen your spirit and make you feel like you're not enough or you're not capable. Instead, see it as a push to do something different, something better.

Rather than assuming that there's sunshine on the other side, believe there's already sunshine where you are. Find your sunshine! This mindset will train you to manage your problems with a happy heart. You can even start enjoying times of problem-solving or challenges because after accomplishing them, the feeling of achievement is rewarding.

Being positive doesn't mean that you wouldn't encounter challenging situations. Your troubles might even get worse. However, when they come, you'll get over them quickly. You'll learn to find the little things that make you happy in your work and personal life.

I worked in an organization where I was really busy. While my colleagues from other departments could relax, I was busier than ever. My team and I needed to fix a problem once, it was nobody's mistake, but we needed to find solutions quickly.

I've always believed in my abilities, but that period was almost an exception. A lot of things were at stake. That was about a massively profitable client. The fact that I might lose my job because of a mistake gave me a lot of headaches. I knew I would get a solution, but I felt like it was a million miles away.

At one point, I wanted to give up. I almost told my team members that it was impossible to solve the issue. Nothing was going right. It seemed like fate was playing some cruel tricks on me.

I couldn't solve the problem, and the managers blamed my department and me. I was devastated. Nothing was going right. I called my best friend to tell him what had happened. He encouraged me and told me to move on and search for another job that would give me more credibility, lifting up my qualities, because that issue was not my fault, and maybe the best expert in the city wouldn't be able to solve it too!

Despite being just a couple of sentences from him, they poured over me and shocked all the senses of my body. A calmness was hardwired into me immediately. That reminded me that my value as a professional depends on me, not anyone else.

No external part of me had changed. What changed was my mentality. Those words warmed my heart and helped me to bounce back. The problem at my former workplace was the push I needed to work somewhere better. I refused to wallow in self-pity and let the loss of my job hold me back, so from that point, I was open to new opportunities. So I used this feeling to unlock my new level of greatness.

Cope With Negative Thinkers

Sometimes, a colleague of mine talks about the government and how societal norms have been unfair to him. Other times, he rants about the corruption that has taken over the hearts of human beings. He makes it seem like there's nothing delightful going on in his life.

He only listens to me speak for a few seconds before interrupting me again. Then, he continues to narrate his tales of woe, and I keep listening. After every conversation we had, I was drained, tired, or frustrated.

Most negative thinkers say negative things because they want more disciples. They don't tell people their problems to get solutions. They just want to rope more people into their misery.

Negative thinkers love sympathy, not solutions! Unfortunately, these people have one thing in common. They carry toxicity that spreads to everyone around them. You might think that you're not affected by negative thinkers. But, their attitude will gradually rub off on you.

Do you notice how you suddenly start complaining about things you would never complain about before? For example, your house suddenly becomes too small, your job too demanding, and your kids too playful. These gloomy complaints will impact your mood, lower your morale and turn you into someone you never wanted to be.

Now, how can you, a positive thinker, cope with negative people if you can't avoid them? How do you maintain a growth mindset without going crazy from all the rants and complaints? How can you find positivity despite all the negativity flying around?

Negative people can be overly sensitive, angry, sad, critical, or rude. However, there's a trick to everything. It's easier to cope with negative thinkers when you try to understand why they act the way they do. Put yourself in their shoes and show empathy.

This does not justify their terrible approach to life and work. It means you're doing your own bit to help them overcome their terrible experience.

Sometimes, negative people aren't aware of how insulting their words are. This is because they're consumed by anger. So, listen without judgment. They may have a crucial point even if it's conveyed unhealthily.

When you respond, don't allow emotions to take charge. Choose your words carefully, and hopefully, it should go smoothly.

Another rule of thumb is to avoid negative energy, so it doesn't affect you. I've realized that I can't fix the people... The best thing I can do is to accept them for who they are and hope they bounce back soon to better reasoning.

What does this mean for you? It means that you can end the conversation after failed efforts to help. Or I could cut short a hangout if the conversation is emotionally draining. Hopefully, they'll develop an appreciative mindset someday. Until then, you can only show empathy while caring for your needs.

If you get to the point of being drained, give yourself a break from a negative thinker. You're not a therapist, so stay away! You also have bad days, and don't go running to burden someone else with your problems all the time. So treat yourself with respect by staying away from negativity if you can't control it.

You don't need to return every text or call immediately. Reach out when you're in the right frame of mind to deal with them. It's OK to have feelings, any sort of emotions. And your emotional condition may vary every day or every few hours. That's completely normal and human!

Spread Positivity To Other People

We live in a world that is constantly full of negativities. These experiences impact our physical and mental health. Many people are struggling to stay sane. Why not be that person that gives others a beacon of hope?

We may not know it, but we all impact one another's life. You can make someone happy today. You can be the reason someone smiles. So start spreading happiness to everyone around you.

Small acts of positivity can change a person's life for good. Be the reason other people believe that their lives can get better. Show that you care. For example, you can give someone a lift in your car if they look too tired to walk or tip the cashier at the grocery store. Small acts of kindness like these help you spread positive vibes and significantly impact others.

When you see a colleague wearing clothes that you love, tell them. Tell your colleagues how beautiful they look that day, how bright their smile is, or how good their attitudes are. Genuine compliments can make a person's day.

Some people need a shoulder to lean on so that they can release negativity out of their system. They want a trustworthy listener to hear them out. Be attentive when someone needs your listening ear. It can make them feel better, just like when someone listens to you when you most need it. And obviously, do it only if you feel willing to.

The 38 Mental Ghosts That Sabotage Our Life Quality

What sabotages our professional activities, social relationships, or relationships at home? Below I state 38 different ghosts that haunt our minds resulting in false beliefs:

1. Shyness and insecurity;
2. Self-punishment;
3. Feeling of guilt;
4. Feeling of revenge;
5. Inferiority complex;
6. Jealousy;
7. Fragmentation of self-esteem;
8. Phobias (social phobia, claustrophobia, technophobia, animal phobia);
9. Low threshold for frustrations;

10. Irritability, impatience and exaggerated emotional fluctuation;
11. Difficulty apologizing and bowing in thanks;
12. Anguish;
13. Impulsivity;
14. Anxiety;
15. Depression;
16. Bad mood;
17. Pessimism;
18. Psychosomatic illnesses;
19. Vigorexia (a psychological problem that causes patients to see themselves as weak and muscleless);
20. Eating disorders (anorexia, bulimia);
21. Chemical dependency;
22. Obsessive Compulsive Disorder (OCD);
23. Conformism;
24. Poorness;
25. Neurotic needs (power, always being right, being the center of attention, talking compulsively);
26. Egocentrism;
27. Individualism;
28. Self-abandonment;
29. Social loneliness;

30. Sabotaging envy;

31. Suffering in anticipation;

32. Rumination of losses and frustrations;

33. Overcharging;

34. Self-collection;

35. Compulsion to Complain;

36. Difficulty in reinventing oneself;

37. Emotional protection deficit;

38. Hypochondria or fear of illness.

Who is afraid to look inwards to look at these emotional ghosts and treat them will be terrified their whole life. It's vital that we make a minimum diagnosis of our limitations, imperfections, difficulties, and performance.

Look At The Silver Lining

Life isn't a bed of roses. Fortunately, many strategies can help you overcome the pains that life brings. One way is to look out for silver linings in every challenging situation.

No matter how bad your day's going, there's always a silver lining in the end. So wake up every morning with a resolve to find the silver lining in your life.

For example, if your employer terminates your employment, the silver lining is that you can try out better opportunities. If your boss condemns your work, the silver lining is that you can try better ways to get it done. The universe may prepare you for something better if your car breaks down. Always search for other positive alternatives in any negative situation.

If your boss gives you a new project, see it as an opportunity for growth. Don't see it as a burden.

When the pandemic hit, everyone was getting laid off, and I was affected too. I knew that the pandemic would last a long time. So, I found ways to stay safe and sent out various applications. Thankfully, I got a remote job that pays well.

I was sad when I was laid off, but I didn't wait for anyone to save me. I found the silver lining myself. You should do that too. Take every bad situation and dig deep to find the good in it.

Practice Gratitude

Gratitude means being thankful for what you have, even if there are many things you don't have. It can improve your mental well-being and solidify your relationships with other people.

Gratitude goes beyond simple politeness, courtesy, or manners. It's about expressing how thankful you are for something.

There's something about practicing gratitude that gives me joy. Whenever I feel down, I start muttering the many things I'm grateful for. And it always works; I always feel better.

Practicing gratitude is like taking a walk in the park; it's a breath of fresh air. The more things you're thankful for, the better life gets.

Recognize and write out the things you are thankful for. Pay attention to the little, routine parts of your life and the positives you may occasionally take for granted.

Having a grateful mind helps you recognize and appreciate your wins, whether big or small. Nothing is too small to be grateful for. You can say "thanks" to a stranger who holds the door for you or be thankful for the rain when it pours.

You can also keep a gratitude diary. Commit yourself to a daily or weekly practice where you recall the people and moments you're grateful for. Afterward, you can try to record them in your diary.

When recording the acts of gratitude in your journal, be specific. Words like "I'm grateful that my colleagues remembered my birthday, and gave me a surprise with a cupcake at work!" will be more effective than "I'm grateful."

Reminiscing how bad things used to be can also teach you gratitude. For example, recalling how hard you worked for small pay and how far you've come will become another reason to be grateful.

Separate Fact From Fiction

The more you brood over negative thoughts, the more control they have over you. Most negative thoughts are not facts. They are mere fictions crafted subconsciously. Your fears are all in your mind; they aren't real. But, they become a cause of concern when you start believing them.

There was a time in my life when I nursed the thought that I was not qualified to apply for a particular role in my dream workplace. I had the requisite academic qualifications and experience. The problem was I doubted my abilities.

I came up with many reasons why I wasn't qualified for the job. However, those roadblocks in my mind were useless because, in reality, I was qualified. I had the certifications and experience required for the job required.

You need to learn to distinguish between what's real and what's an object of your imagination. You can start by writing your thoughts down. Then, read them out aloud and question them. Finally, search for facts that support your thoughts. If you can't find any, then it's probably fiction.

For example, if your mind says, 'they don't like you, say, 'what if they like me? 'or, 'what shows that they don't like me? Once you've taken a moment to analyze your negative thoughts, you will be more objective in evaluating their veracity, and you will be able to choose if you will get affected by a certain emotion or not.

Don't let the imagination of your mind be driven by negative thoughts and ruin your day. Refute those self-defeating thoughts anytime they cross your mind.

I mean it, it works! Practice the 28 days of exercise to break through the way other people affect you.

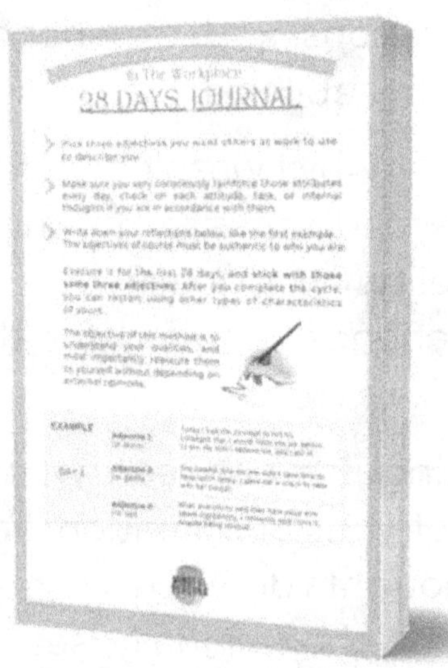

Meditation won't fix all your problems in life, despite being an excellent tool for mind and body awareness. In fact, it may reduce stress, minimize workplace anxiety and improve your sleeping pattern. But bear in mind that It won't get you a new job or pay your bills. It also won't make you fully aware of how your emotions affect you. The 28 Days Worksheet Journal Exercise is a game-changer. It has even better effects when you practice it consistently till the end.

If you'd like to Download The 28 Days Worksheet Journal Exercise at no cost at all, **Click Here**, or access it on my blog's home page:

www.mindfulpersona.com

Combining this exercise with meditation will teach you how to identify and sieve out negative thoughts. It'll help you find positive qualities in yourself by encouraging you to slow down and allow for greater self-reflection.

Meditation is easier than most people think. Find a quiet place and take a seat. You should set a time limit when you're about to start.

Ten minutes a day is an excellent start for a meditation exercise. Take five deep breaths and clear your thoughts. Forget all the work you have left, and just breathe. Make sure you sit in a comfortable position. Close your eyes. Then breathe deeply in and out, focus on emptying your mind, on feeling your body and the intrusive thoughts.

At some point, your mind will wander. Make sure you redirect your mind to where you want it to be. This simple practice will help you to find a healthy balance in life.

Move More, Exercise More, And Improve Your Mood

It's not enough to care for your mental health; your physical health is important too. It'll be hard to have positive thoughts if you're tired and ill.

You need to embrace a healthy lifestyle. Regular exercise can improve mood and minimize stress. It also increases life span and reduces the risk of heart disease. You can set aside 30 minutes or less on most days of the week to exercise.

You can build a healthy diet, nothing radical, to recharge your body. Foods such as yogurt, bananas, oats, dark chocolates, and berries can boost your mood. Lots of water and healthier foods have a positive reaction in our body. You can set a day of the week to eat that junk and deliciously tasty food you like so much. By creating this balance, your body will respond in an amazing way to your mood and brain functionalities.

Don't forget to have lots of water during the day, and sleep well. Also, don't drink alcohol or smoke excessively to prevent mental and physical illnesses. You don't need to cut it off radically but moderately. It's all about a balance of consumption.

Focus On Yourself

You can't give what you don't have. It's not enough to spread positivity to other people. It should start with you. Do you treat yourself with love and respect?

Take care of yourself. Cultivate positive thoughts about yourself and other people.

Sometimes, you can take a break during the day to evaluate your thoughts. If most of your thoughts are negative, you should find sweet spots. For example, "I can tackle it from a different perspective" are more optimistic than "It's too complicated. I can't handle it anymore."

You can't give love if you don't love yourself. So take some time off and go to the beach; get in touch with nature. Get yourself a treat and sleep in on the weekend. I tried these things myself and felt less stressed and more productive at work. Give yourself moments of joy.

Give yourself the license to smile often, even when the times are tough. Don't say hurtful things to yourself. Say no to practices that dampen your spirit. Most importantly, learn to forgive yourself for mistakes in the past. Forgiving yourself and accepting your current version is game-changing.

By engaging in activities that make you feel good, you're transferring your focus from others to yourself.

Finally, the road to positive thinking is not a fast one. It takes determination and consistent practice. Be patient and focus on the small steps that bring you closer to your ultimate goal. Protect your mind from negativity and put yourself first.

When you have an optimistic mindset, you'll become better and make others feel better. So, work on yourself and stay away from things that trigger negative thoughts.

Chapter Ten: The Part To True Healing: Keep A Room For Better Days

"You have the power to heal your life, and you need to know that. We think so often that we are helpless, but we're not. We always have the power of our mind. Claim and consciously use your power."

Louise L. Hay

We all have wounds!

We've been scarred physically, emotionally, and in other ways. You've probably experienced pain that still makes you shiver whenever you remember it. However, to move on, you must allow yourself space to heal. You can't keep holding on to those things that hurt you.

Give yourself time to heal. With time come new opportunities, moments, memories, and healing.

Life continues to give us the time we need. What you use that time for, however, can determine if you'll get the healing you want.

People say that time heals all wounds. But, this isn't true for emotional wounds. These wounds are deeply rooted in our minds. They control the way we act, react and make decisions. So, while time is of the essence, you might also need to speak up to get healing.

Opening up about such a mental struggle might not be as easy as it sounds. You could start by speaking to a friend or a family member about your feelings. But you should also know that their opinions could be subjective. Their judgment might be biased because of the relationship you have.

A therapist, however, has neither personal interests nor assumptions about you. Therefore, you can rely on them to keep your information private and provide you the freedom to express yourself freely to get an honest opinion.

Therapy sessions might take a chunk of your pocket, but they're worth it. It is actually an investment in your life, and your mental health, giving you new chances to live with joy and peace of mind. You get to talk to someone about any minor problems you may be experiencing and learn how to resolve them quickly.

The Importance Of Therapy

The problem with healing is that many people don't even realize they need it. I didn't think I needed to heal too. I thought trauma was something you outgrow. Alas! I was wrong.

If you don't give yourself the time to heal appropriately, trauma will stick with you and direct your life for as long as you live. A few years ago, with the aid of a therapist, I understood that some of my earlier childhood experiences were traumatic. Since then, I've made significant signs of progress toward healing.

Perhaps you were taught that we shouldn't discuss internal struggles. You were taught to keep them as secrets because talking about our problems worsened them, and we become vulnerable by doing that! Vulnerability is seen as a bad position to stay in. But I can't stress enough how flawed and wrong this affirmation is.

I remember someone telling me he could never open up to anybody, not his wife, children, or anyone. His dad taught him that telling people about your life leaves you vulnerable to them. To him, it was a weakness. I can only imagine how others have this orientation. I'm sure many of you reading this book have the same thought.

Speaking up isn't a bad idea! Therapy isn't for weak people. It takes strength to accept that you need help and go for it. It takes even more courage to face your fragilities! So many people become suicidal and fall into depression because they have so much bottled up in their minds. They have no one to talk to and nowhere to pour out all their worries.

A significant benefit of therapy is that it aids honest communication. Most people held within the confines of psychological and emotional trauma do so because they don't speak up. Therapy provides the opportunity for you to speak to a professional. This professional's responsibility is to listen and carry a part of your burden and give you possible solutions and advice.

Therapy is a way to release pent-up thoughts inside you. Therapy can help to:

- Realize and discuss work habits you should and would like to change.
- Handle your relationships better.
- Develop ways of coping with different situations.
- Become self-aware and reflect more on who you are, who you think you are, and who you think others think you are.

- Work and change your perspective and outlook on others.
- Physical symptoms resulting from psychological trauma, such as self-harm, get treated in therapy.
- Find reasons why you feel some emotions in specific moments.
- Connect your past with your current beliefs to talk through them.

Why Should I Do Therapy If I'm Not the Problematic One At Work?

You're probably not the troublesome employee. You're the calm, cool-headed coworker that everyone likes and respects. However, you work with toxic people who try to rub their toxicity on you. They're constantly in your space, and you can't avoid them because you're paid to work together. If this sounds like you, then you still need therapy. Also, therapy is not only for work environment matters; it will work out your whole as a human being to improve your mental health and resilience with the aspects that life brings.

There are so many hurt people in the world today. They're continuously trying to project their fears and insecurities on others. Your resistance to them usually depends on how many coping mechanisms and mental barriers you have built up for yourself.

Many people have carried trauma and pain for so long; it's become baggage for them. They're afraid to open it up because they know that messing with such emotions can refresh events they've tried so hard to forget. So, they try to project their feelings onto others. This is why you might hear a lazy coworker call you 'lazy.'

When your coworker constantly calls you 'lazy,' it begins to sink into your subconscious. The way you think of yourself starts changing. Gradually, you begin to believe that you're lazy.

Therapy helps you protect yourself from the negativity of your coworkers. It acts like a shield of protection that doesn't let negative thoughts go in to attack you. You will eventually get in contact with these toxic comments or conversations, but it won't be a burden as before.

Getting Over Resentment

Imagine that your hands are as small as a child's. You have a handful of sand, and your mum wants to give you flowers. What do you do? You open your palms, let the sand fall out, and take the flowers from your mum. Letting go of resentment happens in this way.

Holding on to resentment is like having a handful of sand and refusing to take the beautiful flowers you deserve. You starve yourself of beautiful things, and the other person keeps living. It's like serving a jail term for another person's crime.

It's only normal to feel resentful when people hurt you. But, learning how to move on from hurt, rejection, or humiliation is crucial to personal growth. If you find that you hold on to resentment for too long, it's an indicator that you need to work on yourself too.

Your brain will absorb what you feed it constantly. So, if you dwell on painful incidences and mentally repeat them daily, you're setting yourself up for a mental illness. It's not easy to forgive someone who left you with psychological trauma, but these steps could help you:

- First, find a calm place where you won't be disturbed.
- Sit quietly and close your eyes like you're about to meditate.
- Relax your body and slow down your breathing.
- Imagine you are seated in a dark place like a theater where there's a stage.

- Let the person you resent climb onto that stage. It could be anybody, and it doesn't matter if they're dead or alive.

- On your imaginary stage, visualize and imagine good things happening to this person. Identify what could be of benefit to them and could make them happy and imagine it coming true. Imagine the person's face lit up with a happy smile.

- Keep this image as a memory, stuck in your head like it's real.

- Now let the person exit the stage.

- It's then your turn. Imagine yourself climbing up the same stage.

- Visualize good things happening to you too. Imagine yourself to be at the highest stage of happiness. See yourself happy and smiling. Keep this as a memory as well.

- Repeat this exercise for 28 days with your Journal Exercise. Then, check daily to see how any resentments you might be feeling are gradually fading away.

- Keep a journal. This is highly recommended. A journal helps keep daily track of your progress. Write daily notes and in them, ask yourself these questions: How do you feel about the person now that you've gone through the exercises? In what way can you improve on this technique and further eliminate resentment?

Some people may think it is a silly thing to practice, but this 28-day exercise is powerful! It's done in repetition and consistency. Please don't give up on it after a day or two. You could extend it past 28 days and stretch it over a longer period depending on your track of progress. Also, conduct this exercise in a serene and quiet environment.

Searching For Therapists?

Generally, there are only very few therapists around. So, finding a good therapist that aligns with and understands your plight is tasking. Usually, you can get a therapist near you by searching online. But the therapist usually has only a short bio and a profile picture. So, how do you know you chose the right one for you?

The therapist may be competent and professional. But, their work with you won't be successful until you can connect with their personality. You're unlikely to disclose your deepest thoughts with your therapist if you avoid discussing some topics with them or don't feel comfortable around them. Hence, you may never get to the bottom of your problems.

To get a good match for you, don't be too harsh on choosing, and don't judge any therapist by:

- Gender
- Age
- Religion
- Work experience
- Certifications

These topics above won't determine if your therapist is good for you or not. Even you don't know who is going to be good for you. So let the preconceptions go, and experience the therapists that come across your path. Give it a chance to see how it goes.

You might try a few therapists before finding the one that clicks. Just ensure that you find a therapist that makes you comfortable. That'll make the therapist-client relationship a lot smoother.

It's okay if you change therapists. There are occasions when the patient and the therapist don't click. That's fine too, but you need to give them a considerable chance before you move on to another one.

Cognitive Behavioral Therapy [CBT]

Cognitive behavioral therapy is a popular form of therapy. It's an effective form of psychotherapy, also known as talk therapy. This treatment approach helps people to recognize negative or unhelpful thoughts and behavior patterns.

CBT aims to help you discover and understand how your thoughts and emotions can influence your actions. It focuses on helping people realize that their inner mind plays a significant role in their outlook and behavioral patterns.

CBT is generally helpful for mental health issues but can also be used to manage other stressful life situations. It can help to:

- Manage mental illness symptoms.
- Treat mental illness when medications aren't the best option, or when you do take medications and need to encounter emotional balance.
- Cope with grief or loss.
- Identify ways of dealing with difficult emotions.

- Resolve relationship conflicts and teach better ways of communication.
- Learn to cope with stressful life situations.
- Learn to cope with medical illnesses and manage chronic physical symptoms.
- Learn to overcome emotional trauma relating to abuse or violence.

CBT is a handy therapy tool as it's used to improve a lot of mental health disorders. For example, it helps to relieve depression, anxiety, post-traumatic stress disorder [PTSD], sleep, and eating disorders, among many others.

However, you must know it might be very uncomfortable initially, especially emotionally. CBT needs you to dive into what are usually painful memories that you probably don't want to revisit.

Some sessions will be harder than others. You might cry, get upset, or feel angry too. Sometimes you might feel physically drained too. However, these 'risks' you're exposed to during the therapy sessions are short-termed. They're usually feelings and fears you must deal with to get better.

Working with a skilled therapist who is very good at their job can help you minimize the extent to which you feel these emotions.

Core Concepts Of CBT

CBT is based on the idea that your thoughts influence your emotions, which influence your actions. So it's a three-way channel; thoughts, emotions or feelings, and actions and how they affect each other.

If your thoughts are negative, so will your feelings. Your actions, too, will be negative. For example, you might become sad if you're constantly under pressure to improve at work and keep thinking about how you'd fail at your tasks. This can, in turn, affect your actions, reduce your quality of work, and bring about terrible work performance.

However, CBT believes that you can change these thoughts and behavior patterns. Your therapist will help restructure your negative thought processes into positive ones.

The American Psychological Association [APA] says that there are several core concepts of CBT, including:

- Psychological problems are partly based on unhelpful or unhealthy ways of thinking.

- Psychological problems are partly based on learned patterns of negative behavior.
- People suffering from psychological problems may learn better ways of coping with them. As a result, they can find ways to reduce their symptoms and become more effective in their lives.

These core concepts further show that most mental and psychological struggles you have usually stem from the thoughts you keep in mind. Having negative thoughts can contribute to emotional distress and issues. These thoughts can then lead to negative behavior that becomes a repetitive behavioral pattern over time.

Learning how to change these patterns as soon as they are discovered can help you deal with them and reduce future distress.

Popular CBT Techniques

CBT employs various techniques. It's left to your therapist to determine which techniques work best for you. A typical CBT treatment usually involves:

- Recognizing how inaccurate and unhelpful thoughts can worsen problems.
- Learning new problem-solving skills.

- Gaining confidence and having a better understanding of your self-worth.
- Learning how to face challenges and fears.

However, people are different. So, the techniques that apply to one might not work for the other. Your therapist will determine which technique works best for you.

These techniques aim to replace self-deprecating thoughts with more encouraging, self-appreciating ones. Some popular CBT techniques are:

SMART goals

SMART means specific, measurable, achievable, realistic, and timely. This technique will serve as a guide while setting your goals. In addition, it'll instruct you on how to define your goals or tell them apart from one another.

Setting goals can help you take action to transform your life as you recover from mental illness. Your therapist will assist you in strengthening your goal-setting abilities by using SMART as a guide.

Guided Discovery And Questioning

With this technique, the therapist asks questions about your assumptions about yourself and from what perspective you view yourself. The therapist then challenges these thoughts and helps you consider different viewpoints.

You must know the situation, emotions, and thoughts that lead to behavioral problems. So, taking the time to name these emotions and challenge them can help you uncover who you are and offer new suggestions that are key to your healing process.

Journaling

Keeping notes is a good technique. You could be asked to record negative thoughts weekly, with a follow-up of positive ones that might replace them.

Writing in a journal allows you to recognize and let go of your daily thought patterns. It's therapeutic! Writing down your thoughts helps you make sense of the situation. When we journal our thoughts, they lose their power. This, in turn, reduces the intensity of difficult emotions.

Self-talk

Replacing negative self-talk with positive affirmations trains your mind to believe those good things will happen to you. As a result, you learn to see a complete truth rather than focus on any situation's bad parts.

You're more likely to develop confidence and self-esteem, experience greater control over your life, and succeed in your goals if you speak to yourself positively.

Thought recording

In this technique, you record thoughts and feelings you experienced during a particular situation, then come up with evidence to support your thoughts.

It's like keeping a running log of your actions or experiences and sharing them with your therapist. Your therapist can then get the necessary data and give you the best remedies.

Positive activities

Adding a reasonable amount of rewarding activities to your daily schedule can help lift your mood and increase your positivity. It could be simple activities such as taking a walk in the park on a bright afternoon or buying a few fresh flowers.

Situation Exposure

This involves stating or writing out various situations that cause you to be distressed. Slowly exposing yourself to these situations helps you manage them better when they occur.

You'll also learn relaxation techniques to help you cope with your feelings in difficult situations.

Psychoanalysis

Psychoanalysis is a treatment used in CBT. However, not all therapists use it, but it's one of the most frequently used. It is a theory of mind. It's based on the belief that people possess unconscious thoughts, feelings, and desires. Psychoanalysis aims to awaken these 'repressed' unconscious emotions and experiences. Healing only happens if the person can be helped.

The theory is that you cannot treat or reduce symptoms without dealing with the underlying internal conflict. It thinks that solving an issue is relatively inconsequential without finding out the root cause of the issue and effectively resolving it.

Therapists use psychoanalysis to treat depression and anxiety disorders. The process is usually a long one as it involves the patient being in a relaxed state while telling stories of their past to the therapist, who takes notes. It involves several sessions with the therapist, stretching over the years possibly.

Even before you find a good therapist, you feel comfortable starting a journey of self-awareness and healing and that the professional therapist is not responsible for your actions, attitudes, or decisions. But, they will be there for you, guiding you through your thoughts and helping you clarify how you deal with a particular moment, emotion or situation.

It is like crossing a barrier of fire. It's painful and disturbing sometimes, but it will take you to a different level of understanding of how your mind works and how to control yourself better. Life will get easier as you develop this mental resilience.

Review

198 customer reviews

5.0 out of 5 stars

5 star		99%
4 star		0%
3 star		0%
2 star		1%
1 star		0%

Review this product

Share your thoughts with other customers

Write a customer review

If you've found this book helpful so far, kindly leave me with a 5-star review on Amazon! This will help this book reach more and more people, increasing the chances for a better mentality and mental health in companies worldwide!

Also, Join Our Private Group For

Great Content and Sharings!

MP Therapeutic Writing Support Group

https://www.facebook.com/groups/mpwritingtherapy

This is a private group where you can write whatever makes you pleased, also learn, ask questions, discuss and get valuable content when it comes to improving Emotional and Mental Health.

Writing therapy, otherwise described in the literature as “expressive (emotional) disclosure”, or “expressive writing”, may have the potential to heal mentally and physically.

"I hear and I forget, I see and I remember, I write and I understand." - Proverb

This is a group you will get a lot from, which means you also should give and contribute to the community as well. We encourage you to share your experiences either with unsolved emotional struggles or wins, to inspire and help others with support.

We'll be waiting for you there!

We haven't finished our journey yet, but your review would mean the world to me, as we could reach more readers craving tools to cope with similar situations!

Let's move on.

Conclusion

Well done!

You made it to the end of the book. I must commend you for staying with me till this moment. But before I go, let's quickly recap what we've discussed so far.

You can't leave your workplace, but you still need to cope with the personalities you work with. So, what do you do? Try to listen! A very wise book called Bible cites this scripture: James 1:19 *"Everyone should be quick to listen, slow to speak and slow to become angry."*

The most common human need is to be heard and understood. It isn't any different in the work setting. Employers and employees want to speak and expect others to be quiet and understand. It could lead to a lot of friction in the workplace. So, when you and a coworker are at odds, try to see things from their point of view. Let them speak even if you disagree with what they say. You can learn from the experiences of others.

Also, you should evaluate your performance thoroughly before your supervisor does. For example, what does your employer always complain about? Have you tried to correct it? Are you defensive when corrected? Are you nonchalant about your job? You must check your performance and behavior using your boss' lens.

Do you behave rudely toward others, come in late, waste time chatting with friends rather than working, or use corporate supplies for personal use? Any of these actions will give the impression that you have a bad attitude. So, check yourself first.

If you're sure you're doing everything right, but your bosses never seem satisfied, then don't be scared to speak up. Set up a private meeting where you can speak to your boss personally.

You should talk about your ideas and suggestions and let them know how much effort you've put in. You can also ask for advice on what they want you to do.

Ask your supervisor if your workplace provides training to assist you in learning new skills that might be helpful to your position. If training is not provided, let your employer know that you are looking into all options to improve your performance at work.

The best way to succeed in your workplace is to set goals. Setting goals gives you a vision. You'll know what to work toward and easily decipher when moving off track. Also, it strengthens your weaknesses while pushing you to use your strengths better.

Getting a mentor you love and respect can also help you successfully scale through your workplace. In addition to helping mentees become professionals, mentors also offer emotional support. They can also help build your career by using their connections and influence.

No matter how much you love your job, you're bound to get burned out if you don't get enough rest. Having to deal with loads and work will leave you irritated and stressed. So, losing interest in your job doesn't necessarily mean working with toxic coworkers; maybe you need to slow down.

Take out time to rest. Take a day off to do other things you love; go fishing, hiking, or read a book. You'll go back to work feeling refreshed and ready to do more.

For every success, there's a row of failures behind it. So, don't expect to fly to the top without being ruffled. Your boss could condemn your work and colleagues and spread terrible narratives about you. Don't be startled.

Accept your failure with lots of love and work towards righting the wrongs. It becomes much more difficult for other people to poison you with their toxicity when you are at peace with your choices and attitudes.

For instance, instead of becoming upset or triggered when someone tries to offend you with a terrible comment, you'll feel sad for the offender.

You'll realize how much this coworker must be hurting on the inside, and you'll even try to make them feel better.

Finally, toxic coworkers can't get to you if you don't let them. So, work on loving yourself so much that all the toxicity doesn't bug you.

I hope this book sparked a fire in your mind that burns out negativity and pushes you to do better. I also hope it gives you strong motivation to do better in your workplace. So now that you have all the help you need, go into that work and live your best life.

All the best!

Don't forget to DOWNLOAD your

28 Days Worksheet Journal Exercise

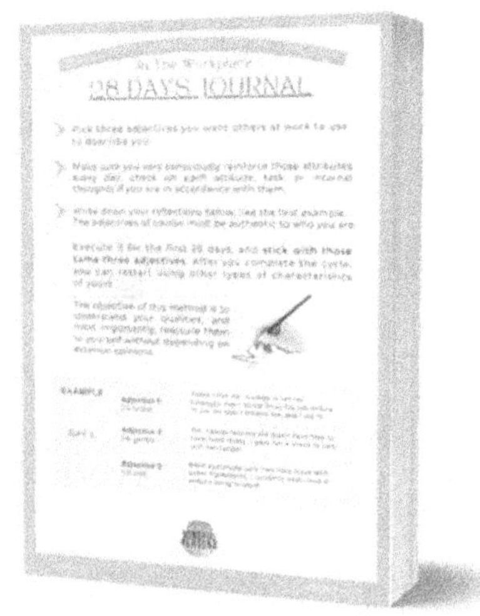

The objective of this method is to understand your qualities, and most importantly, reassure them to yourself without depending on external opinions.

If you'd like to Download
The 28 Days Worksheet Journal Exercise at no cost at all, access it on my blog's home page if you have a Paperback Version of this book:

www.mindfulpersona.com

Get your copy free from charge today.

Resources

Branney, J. (2022, July 5). Workplace Personality Types: How To Manage Different Personalities. *SEFE&MT*. Retrieved October 4, 2022, from https://www.sefe-mt.com/careers/blog/different-personality-types-workplace-use-advantage/

Gail, Carly (2022, July 5) 5 Benefits of Understanding Personalities in the Workplace. (n.d.). Retrieved October 4, 2022, from https://www.crystalknows.com/blog/personalities-in-the-workplace

Robbins, T. (2021, March 24). How to work with different personalities | Tony Robbins. tonyrobbins.com. Retrieved October 4, 2022, from https://www.tonyrobbins.com/leadership-impact/working-with-different-personalities

Fishbein, R. (2021, December 7). Tricks for Dealing With Toxic Colleagues - Office Politics. Medium. Retrieved October 4, 2022, from https://medium.com/s/office-politics/tricks-for-dealing-with-toxic-colleagues-fc19677300d6

Krumina, K. (2022, August 23). Career goals – 30 examples & how to set them | DeskTime Blog. DeskTime Insights. Retrieved October 4, 2022, from https://desktime.com/blog/career-goals-30-examples-and-how-to-set-them

York, J. (n.d.). Is HR ever really your friend? BBC Worklife. Retrieved October 4, 2022, from https://www.bbc.com/worklife/article/20211022-is-hr-ever-really-your-friend

Wilkie, D. (2019, August 16). Workplace Gossip: What Crosses the Line? SHRM. Retrieved October 4, 2022, from https://www.shrm.org/resourcesandtools/hr-topics/employee-relations/pages/office-gossip-policies.aspx#:%7E:text=Some%20negative%20consequences%20of%20workplace,is%20and%20isn't%20fact.+https://iveybusinessjournal.com/publication/the-tyranny-of-toxic-managers-an-emotional-intelligence-approach-to-dealing-with-difficult-personalities/

Fernandes, T. (2022, January 7). The Difference Between Mentors, Sponsors, and Advisors. Medium. Retrieved October 4, 2022, from https://medium.com/pm101/the-difference-between-mentors-sponsors-and-advisors-184f11499382

EVA, A. (2017, May 4). How to Stay Empathic without Suffering So Much. *Greater Good Magazine*. Retrieved October 4, 2022, from https://www.scribbr.com/citation/generator/folders/3nquIXAVETt1qtzAZ8Fy9d/lists/5FjDuJ5cdzxgTgc0miQ6Kj/cite/online-news-article/

Buckley, D. (2022, August 30). Can Self-Punishment Be A Tool For Improvement? | BetterHelp. Retrieved October 4, 2022, from https://www.betterhelp.com/advice/behavior/can-self-punishment-be-a-tool-for-improvement/

Henley, D. (2018, December 14). What To Do When You Feel Like You Are Failing At Work. Forbes. Retrieved October 4, 2022, from https://www.forbes.com/sites/dedehenley/2018/12/14/what-to-do-when-you-feel-like-a-failure-at-work/?sh=2edbba532b9c

www.ingramcontent.com/pod-product-compliance
Lightning Source LLC
Chambersburg PA
CBHW020458030426
42337CB00011B/150

* 9 7 8 1 7 3 9 1 7 1 0 1 8 *